IMPROVE YOUR
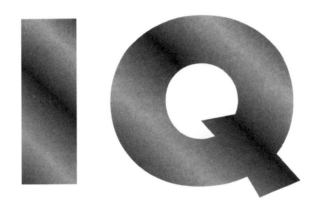
IQ

IMPROVE YOUR

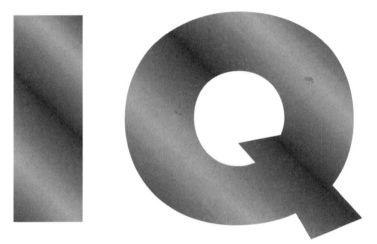

Over 500
Mind -Bending Puzzles

Edited by Deborah Hercun

BARNES
&NOBLE
BOOKS
NEW YORK

IMPROVE YOUR IQ

is a baffling, mind-stretching, entertaining and sometimes infuriating test of your mental abilities.

These puzzles are designed to challenge your powers of deduction and logic, but they also ask you to think laterally and imaginatively.

the book is carefully designed into sections of ascending difficulty and it is important that you work through the book as it is laid out. If you go straight to the puzzles in section 10, you may end up tearing your hair out; however, if you tackle them having mastered the previous chapters, they will begin to make sense.

It can be an almost irresistible temptation to turn to the answers before you have worked out your own solution. Please persevere - your patience will be rewarded. If you get the answer wrong, go back over the problem until you finally see how the answer was arrived at. As the book unfolds, by properly appreciating the earlier answers, they will act as stepping-stones to help you solve more complicated puzzles.

Try to think laterally. A key to solving problems can be to tackle them from a fresh or unexpected angle. You can only benefit by approaching problems with a different perspective.

Puzzle solving can be one of the most amusing and entertaining pastimes as well as helping you to sharpen your wits and train you to think more clearly.

Improve your IQ will provide you with hours of challenging fun. You may also discover that your mental powers and your IQ are more impressive than you ever imagined. And problem solving is of use wherever we find ourselves.

1

Which of the six numbered shapes goes in the empty square?

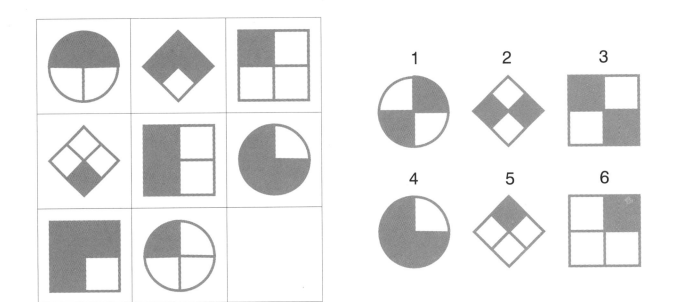

2

Which number starts this sequence?

?
9
16
25
36

3

Can you fill in the blanks?

C	L
M	D
?	?
O	F
G	P
Q	H

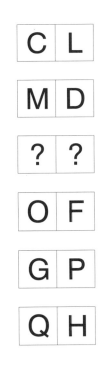

4

Can you insert the missing numbers?
(A different rule applies to each box.)

A

9	15	21
3	5	?

B

9	12	20
2	5	?

C

4	16	24
2	8	?

5

Which letter is the odd one out in each circle?

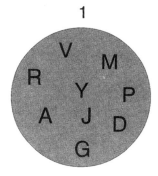

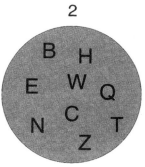

6

Can you fill in the blanks?

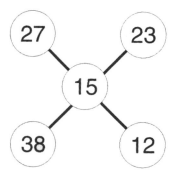

A

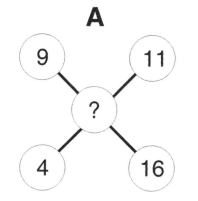

B

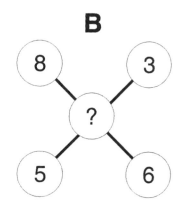

- 8 -

7

Can you insert the missing number?

8

Can you move these matches and change the number to sixteen?

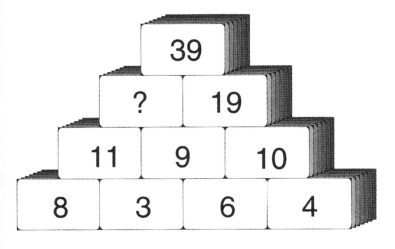

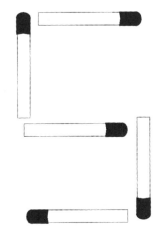

9

All of these pieces, except one, will form a square when correctly replaced back into the grid. Can you work out which is the extra piece?

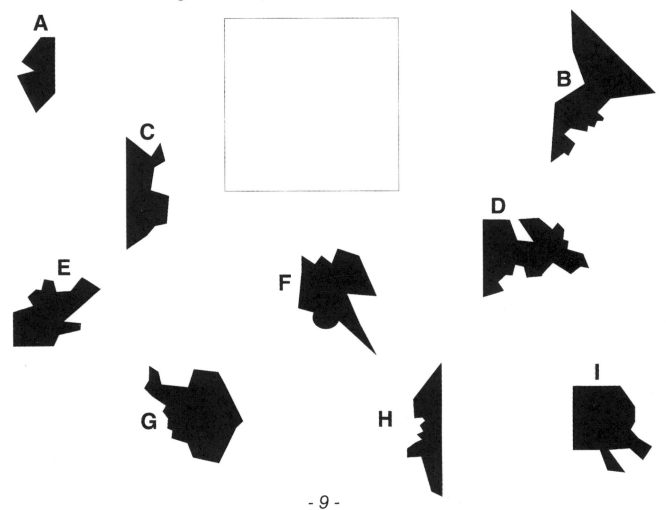

10

Which of these six watches should replace the blank one?

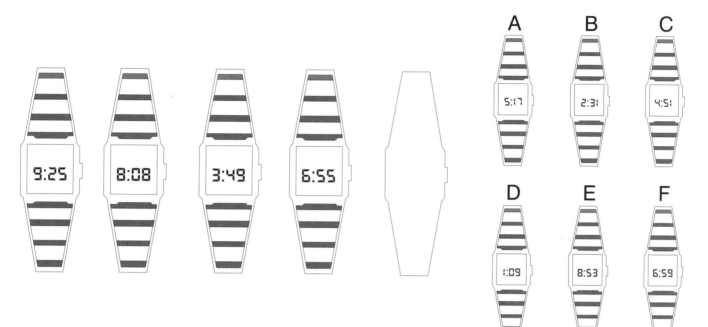

11

Can you fill in the blank?

B

E

I

L

P

?

W

12

Can you work out which number is missing?

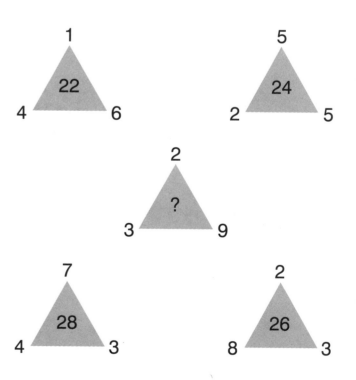

13

Which of the five numbered pieces goes in the shaded area?

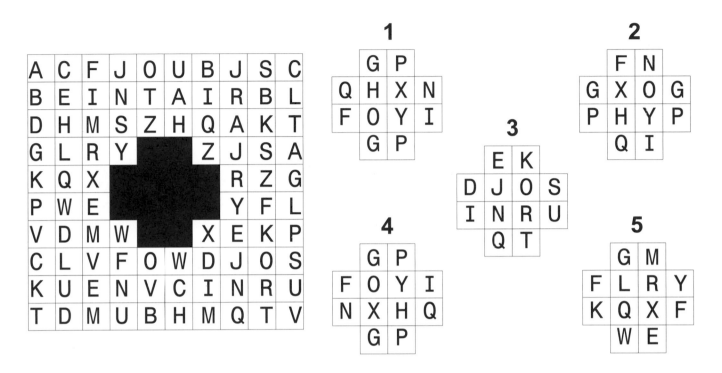

1

G	P		
Q	H	X	N
F	O	Y	I
	G	P	

2

	F	N	
G	X	O	G
P	H	Y	P
	Q	I	

3

	E	K	
D	J	O	S
I	N	R	U
	Q	T	

4

G	P		
F	O	Y	I
N	X	H	Q
	G	P	

5

	G	M	
F	L	R	Y
K	Q	X	F
	W	E	

14

Solve this riddle

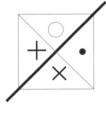

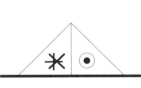

A   is to   **B**   as   **C**   is to

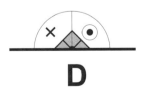

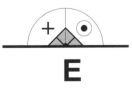

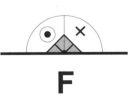

D   **E**   **F**

15

Which statement is wrong?

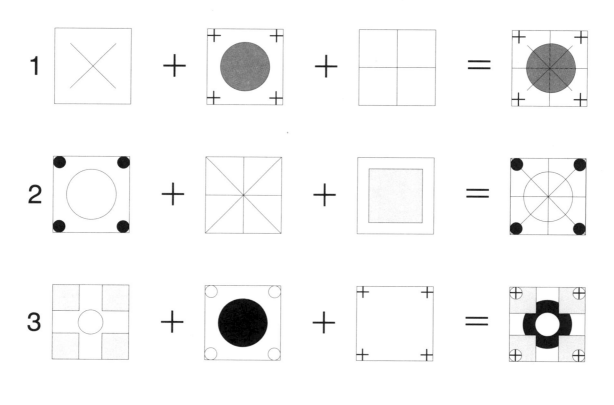

16

*Finishing at the square with a star in it -
can you find the start point in this grid?*

*Move one square North when
you land on a square marked N1,
two squares South when you land
on a square marked S2 etc. etc.*

2S	2S	1W	2E	4W	1S
4S	2S	2E	2W	3W	5W
2E	2E	2S	3S	1N	★
2E	2S	1N	2N	1W	5W
1N	2E	3E	2W	4N	1W
2E	3E	5N	2E	2N	3N

17

Draw two straight lines through the box to end up with four sections, each containing three of each symbol.

18

If a dog is worth 5, can you work out what the other symbols are worth?

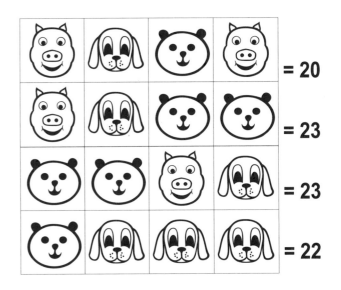

= 20

= 23

= 23

= 22

19

Can you work which letter is missing?

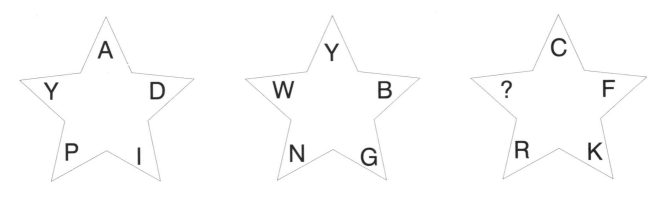

A
Y   D
P   I

Y
W   B
N   G

C
?   F
R   K

20

Can you work out which number is missing?

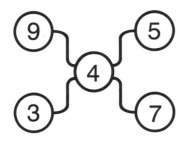

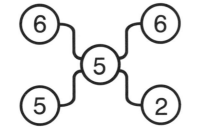

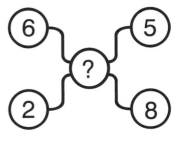

9   5
4
3   7

6   6
5
5   2

6   5
?
2   8

21

Which of the six numbered pieces
will complete the sequence?

22

One of the following statements
is incorrect - which one?

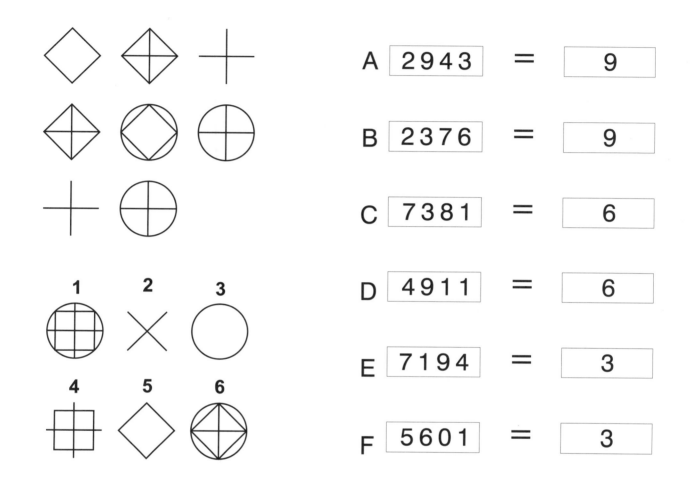

A [2 9 4 3] = [9]

B [2 3 7 6] = [9]

C [7 3 8 1] = [6]

D [4 9 1 1] = [6]

E [7 1 9 4] = [3]

F [5 6 0 1] = [3]

23

Can you work out which number is missing?

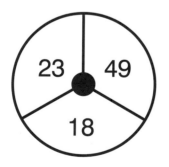
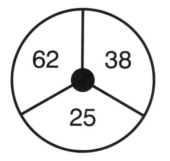
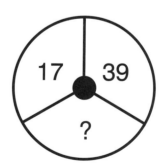

24

Can you insert the missing numbers?

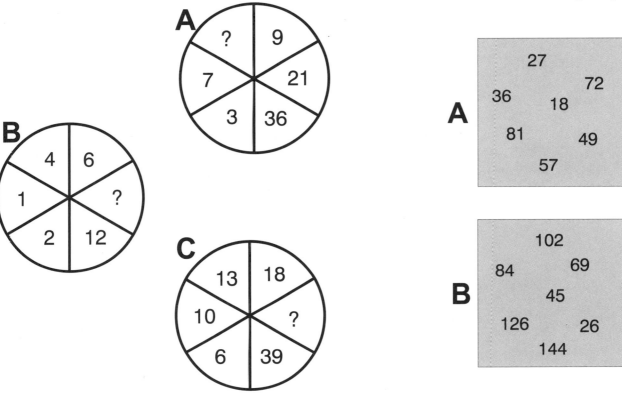

25

Which number is the odd one out in each group?

A

27
72
36   18
81   49
57

B

102
84   69
45
126   26
144

26

Which symbol continues this sequence?

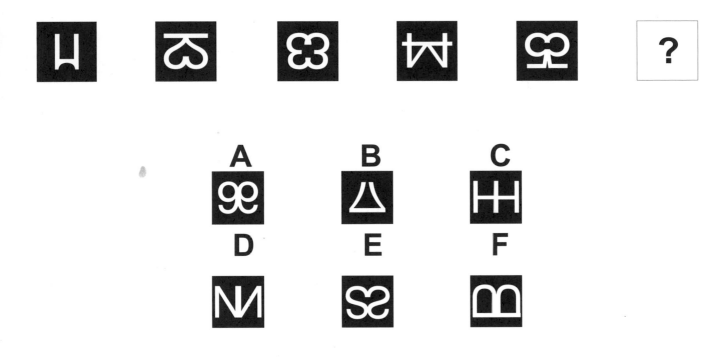

27

Which of the six numbered figures completes the sequence?

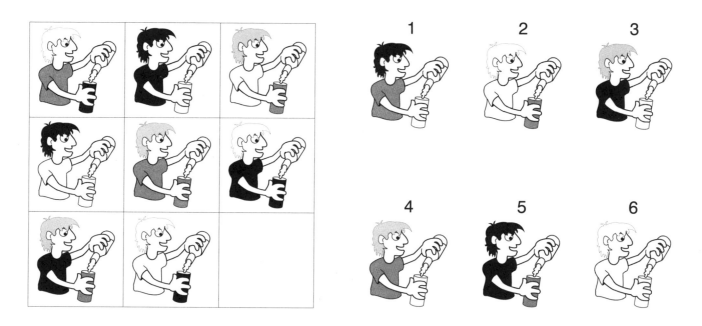

1   2   3

4   5   6

28

Can you work out which is the missing letter in each wheel?

1

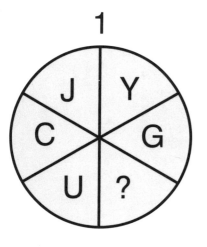

J Y
C G
U ?

2

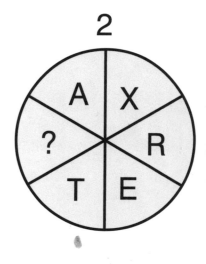

A X
? R
T E

3

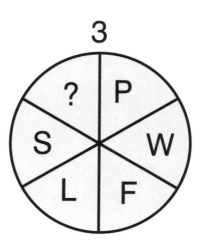

? P
S W
L F

1

By following the same rule as used in each of the first four circles, can you complete the fifth circle?

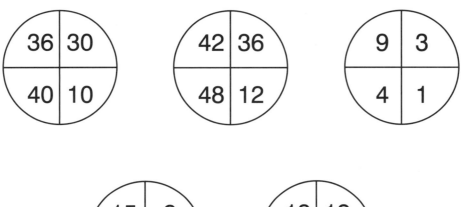

2

Which letter is missing?

3

Can you replace the question mark?

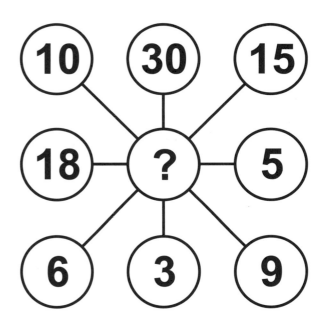

4

Which number completes the puzzle?

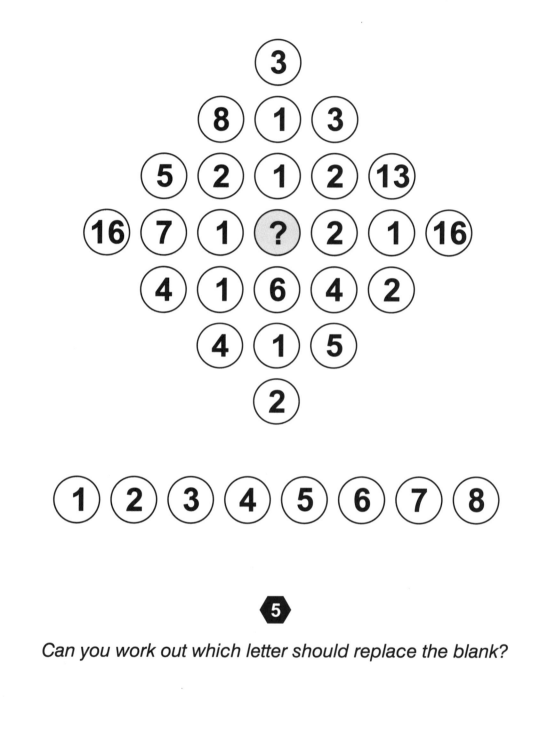

5

Can you work out which letter should replace the blank?

6

Which letter completes the sequence?

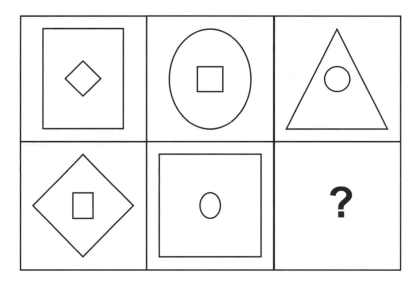

7

Add the correct number to the empty box.

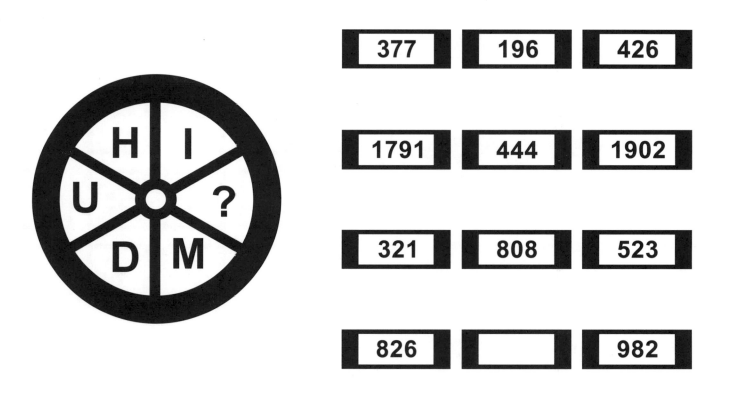

377	196	426
1791	444	1902
321	808	523
826		982

8

Which shape continues this sequence?

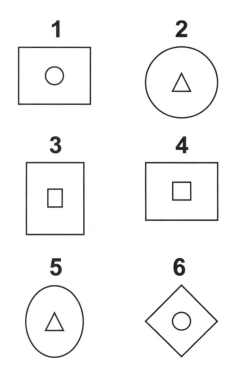

1 2 3 4 5 6

9

Which letter should replace the blank?

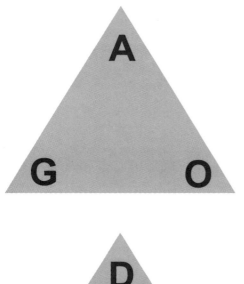

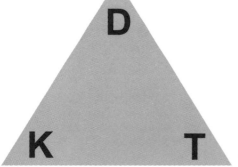

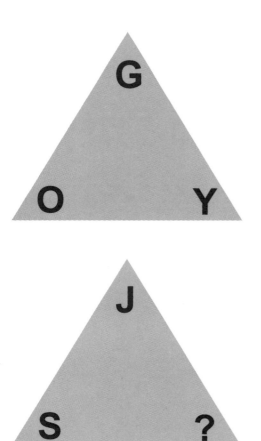

10

Can you fill in the blank?

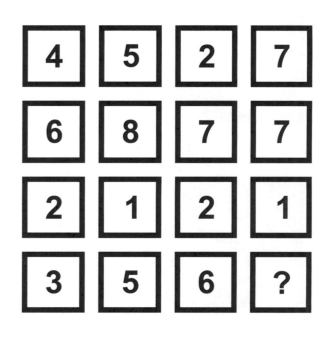

4	5	2	7
6	8	7	7
2	1	2	1
3	5	6	?

11

Which letter completes the sequence?

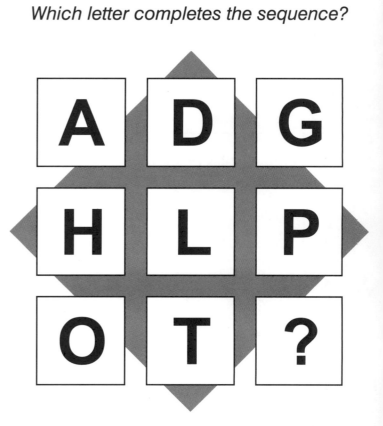

A	D	G
H	L	P
O	T	?

12

Which is the odd one out?

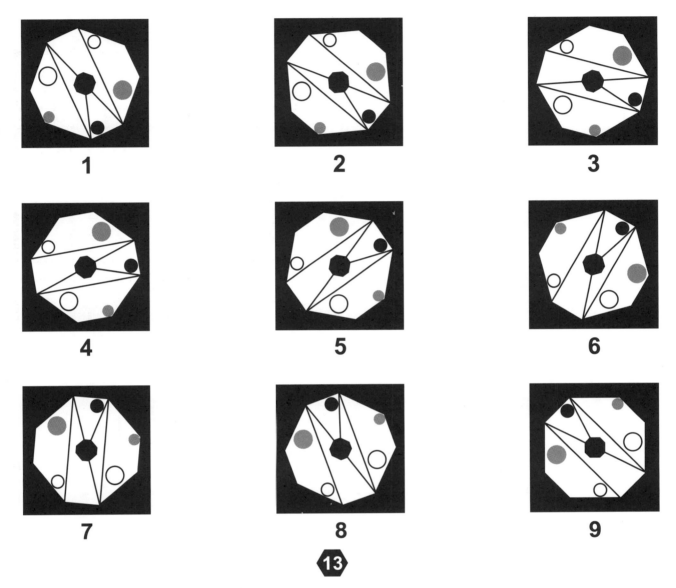

13

By using the same rule for each puzzle - can you fill in the missing numbers?

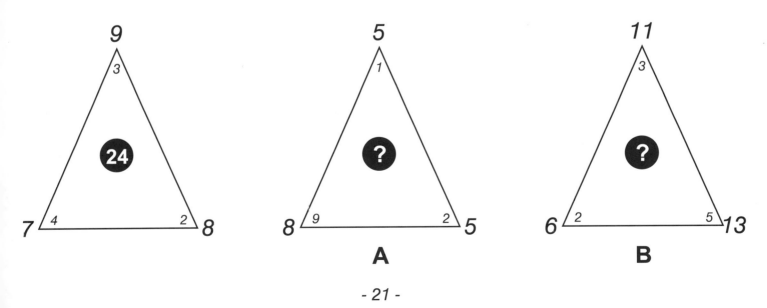

14

Can you fill in the blank?

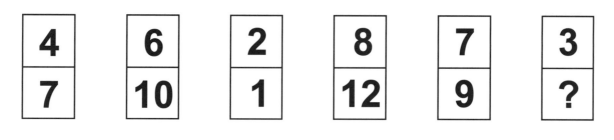

15

Which square continues the sequence?

 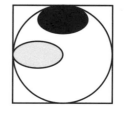

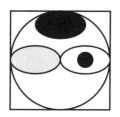 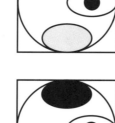 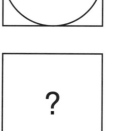

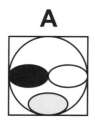 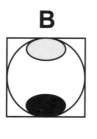 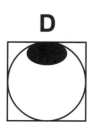

A
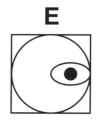

B
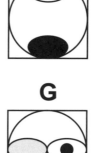

C

D

E

F

G

H
 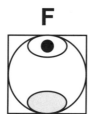 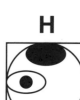

16

Can you replace the question mark?

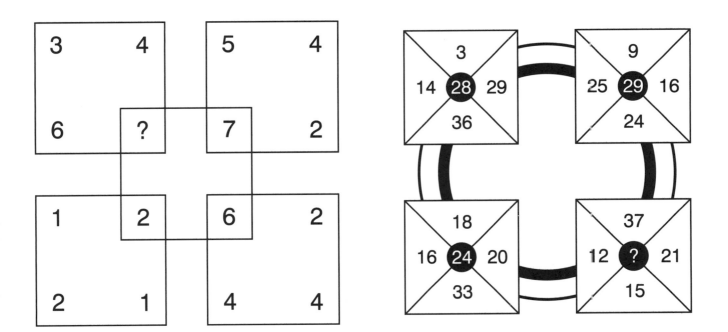

3	4
6	?

5	4
7	2

1	2
2	1

6	2
4	4

17

Can you find the missing number?

3
14 28 29
36

9
25 29 16
24

18
16 24 20
33

37
12 ? 21
15

18

Which of the six numbered boxes completes the sequence?

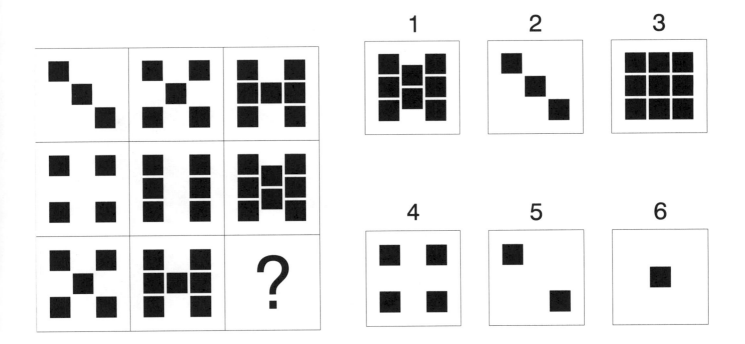

1   2   3

4   5   6

19

Which shape continues the sequence?

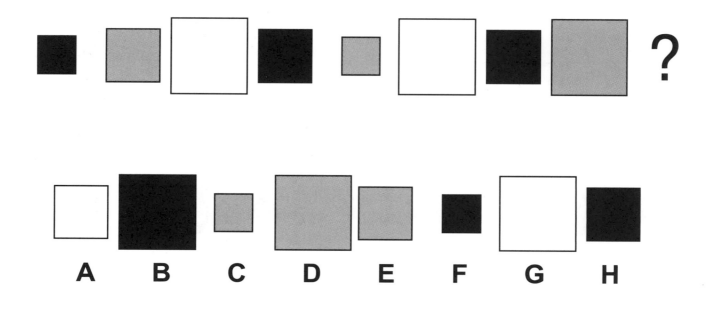

20

Which letter replaces the blank and completes the sequence?

21

Can you replace the missing number?

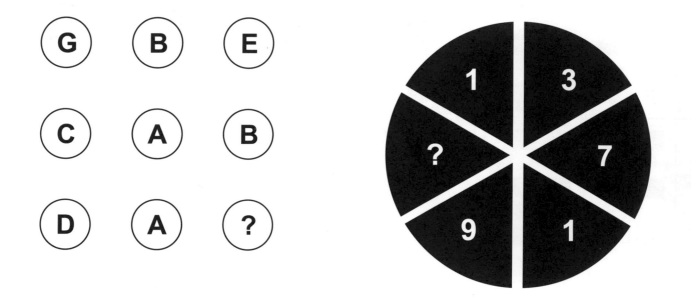

22

Which letter replaces the blank and completes the chain?

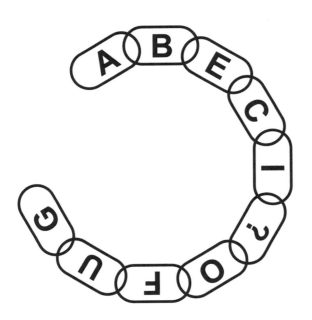

23

Can you replace the missing number?

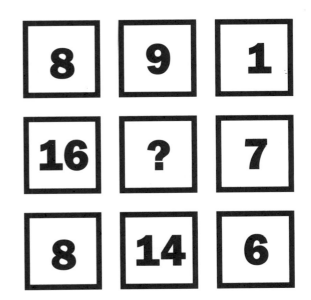

24

Which letter replaces the blank?

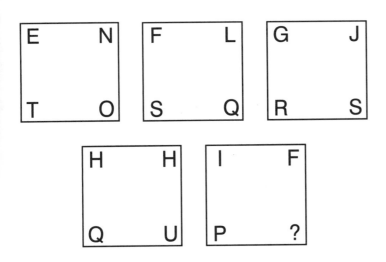

25

Can you complete the sequence?

26

Can you solve this teaser?

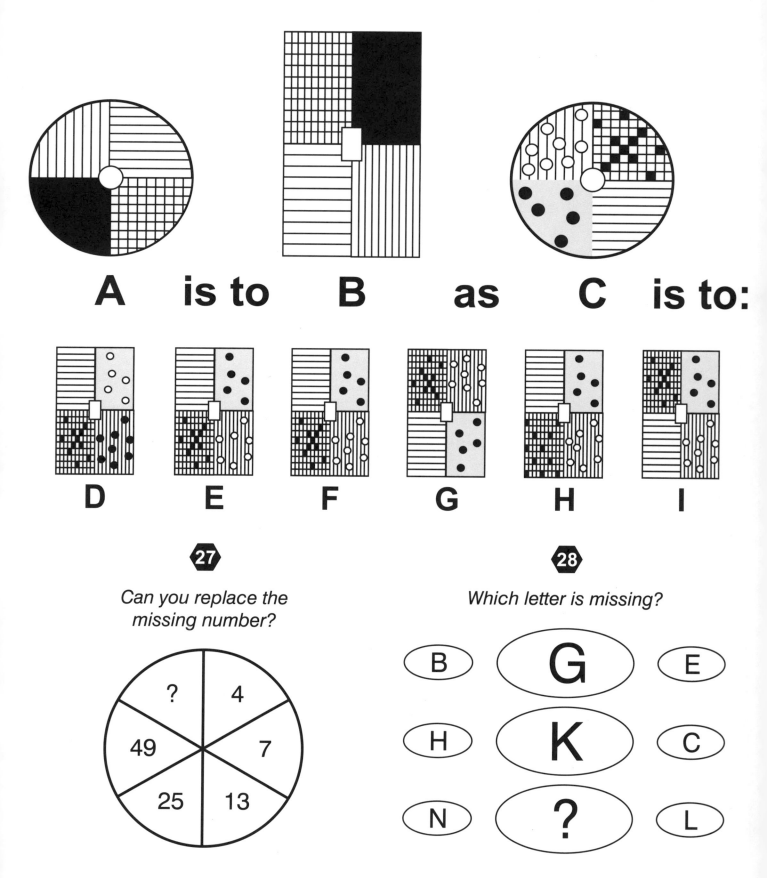

A   is to   B   as   C   is to:

D   E   F   G   H   I

27

Can you replace the missing number?

? | 4
49 | 7
25 | 13

28

Which letter is missing?

B   G   E

H   K   C

N   ?   L

Which cube can be formed by folding this shape?

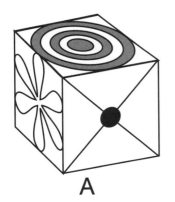

A

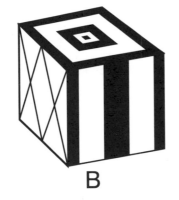

B

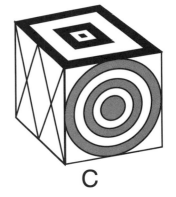

C

D

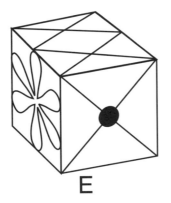

E

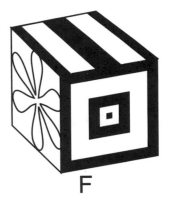

F

2

Which of the four numbered shapes completes the sequence?

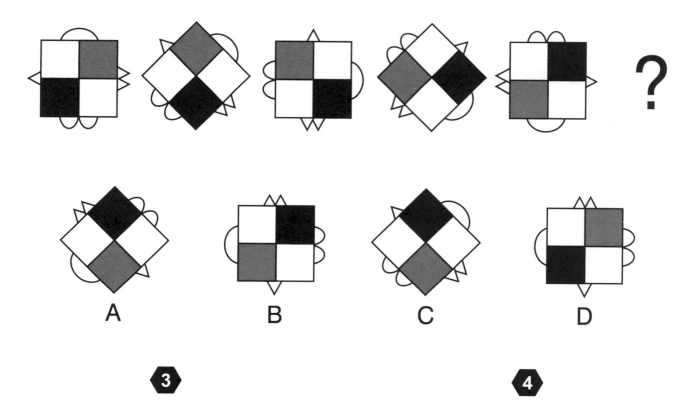

A   B   C   D

3

A man was in a burger bar one day. When he had finished his meal he drew the following picture in green ink on his bill:

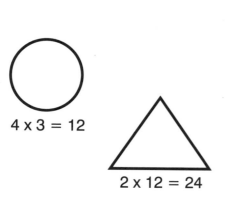

2 x 13 = 26

4 x 3 = 12

2 x 12 = 24

As he handed the bill to the waitress with his money she said to him "You're in the Navy aren't you?" How did she know?

4

Can you replace the missing letter?

5

Replace all the numbers so that each row, column and diagonal adds up to 23

6

What does 6 equal?

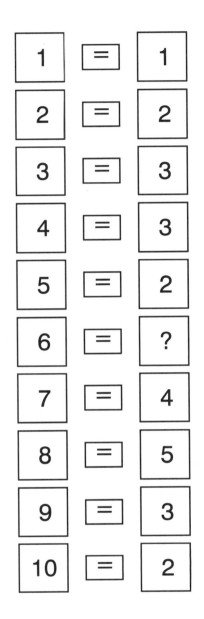

1	=	1
2	=	2
3	=	3
4	=	3
5	=	2
6	=	?
7	=	4
8	=	5
9	=	3
10	=	2

7

Which letter is missing?

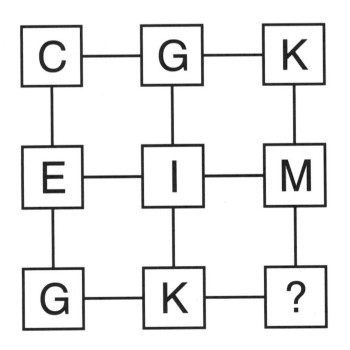

8

Can you explain why these answers are correct?

A - 7 x 6 x 3 = 9

B - 3 x 2 x 9 = 9

C - 7 x 3 x 3 = 9

D - 17 x 6 x 3 = 9

9

Can you complete the wheels?

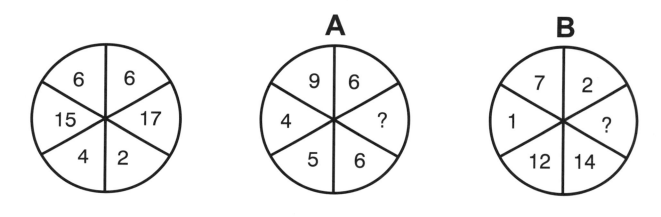

A

B

10

Can you write in the correct letters to continue this sequence?

   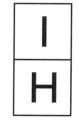 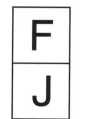 

R	O	?	I	F	C
B	D	?	H	J	L

11

Which card replaces the blank one?

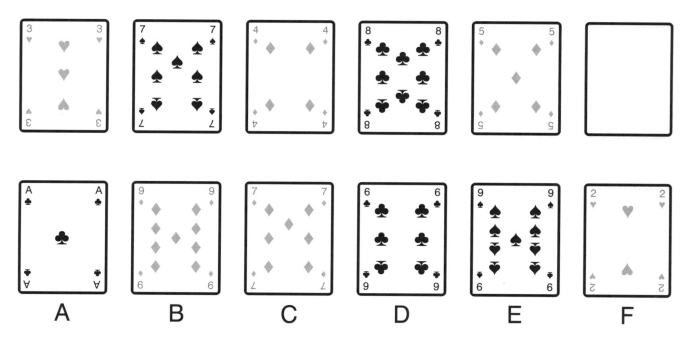

A   B   C   D   E   F

12

Which letter replaces the blank and completes the sequence?

13

Can you complete this number square?

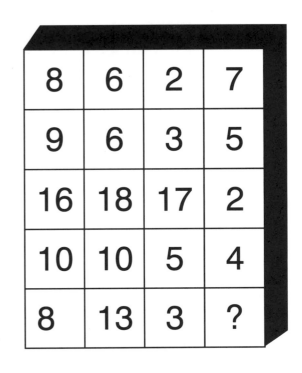

14

Can you fill in the blanks?

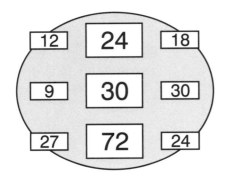

A

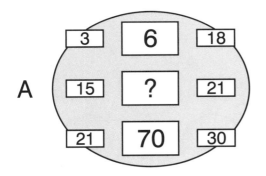

B

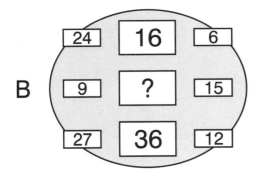

15

Study the example puzzles and, by using the same rule, can you complete the last puzzle?

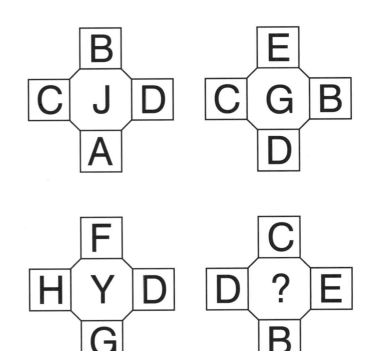

16

Which flag is the odd one out?

A

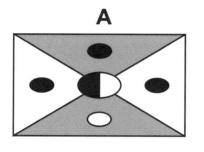

B

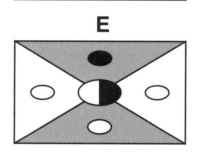

C

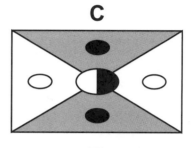

D

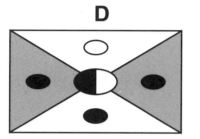

E

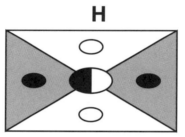

F

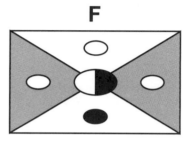

G

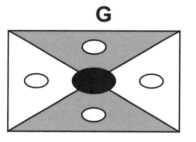

H

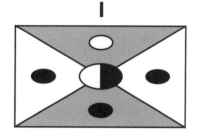

I

17

Which number is missing?

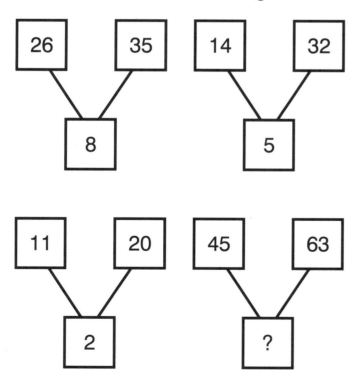

18

Which letter is missing?

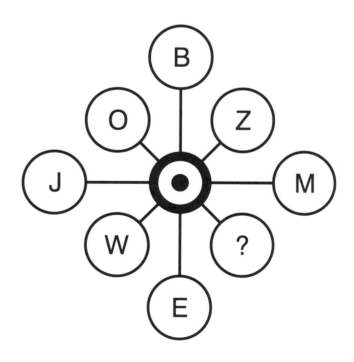

LEVEL 3

19

By following the example given, can you complete the other two puzzles?

1 **2**

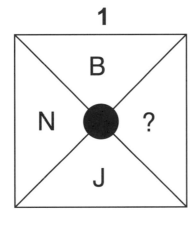

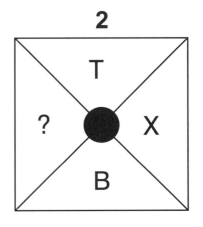

20

Can you work out what should go in the blanks?

A **B** **C**

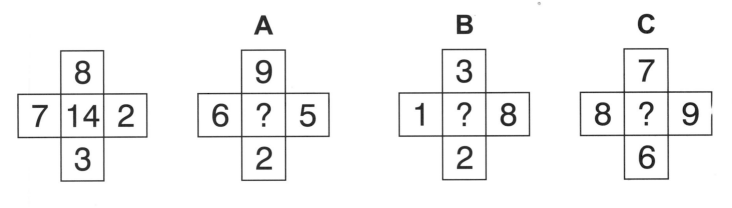

21

Which letter should replace the blank?

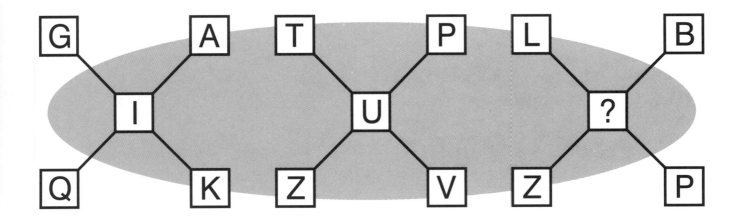

- 33 -

22

Which number is missing?

7	14
91	35

3	2
19	7

6	9
63	24

8	7
?	22

23

Which letter is missing?

F J
K
L P

L X
S
N Z

B M
?
A L

24

Which square continues this sequence?

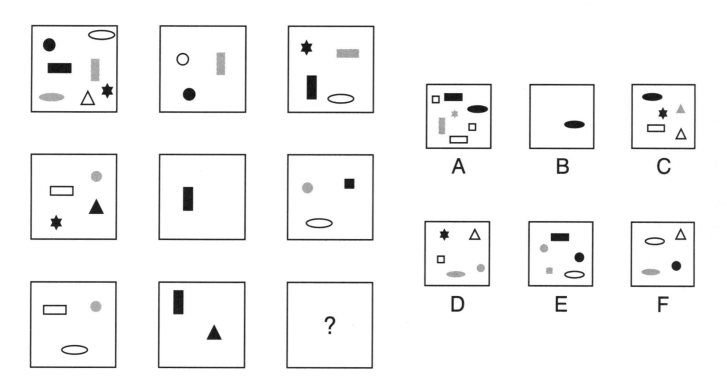

A B C

D E F

25

Which number is missing?

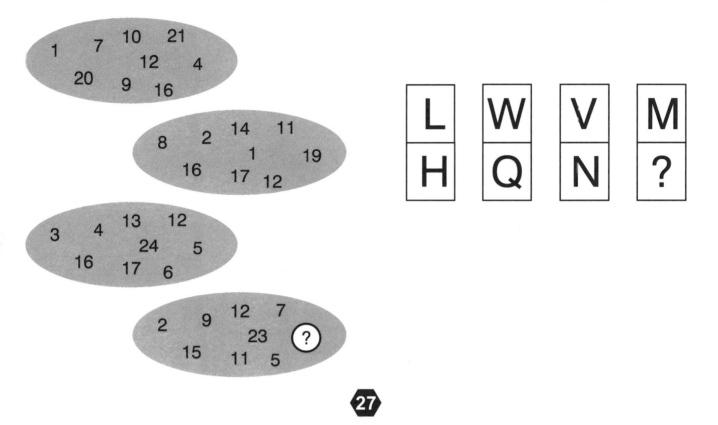

26

Which letter replaces the blank and completes the sequence?

L	W	V	M
H	Q	N	?

27

Which square replaces the empty one?

A   B   C

D   E   F

G   H   I

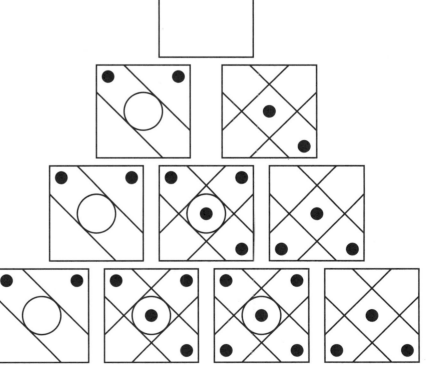

28

What time should the blank clock show?

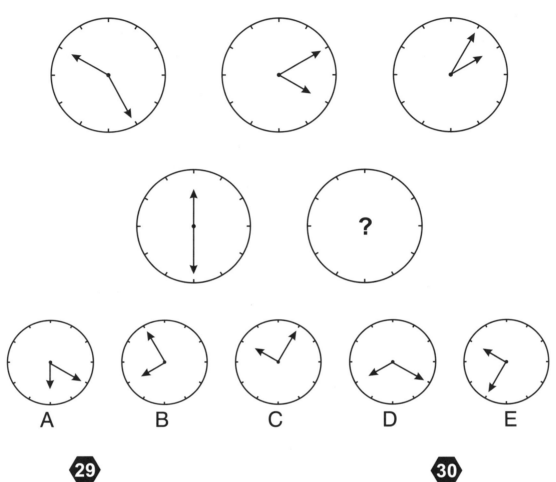

A B C D E

29

Can you complete these puzzles using the example given?

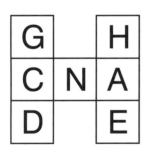

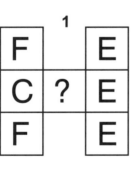
1

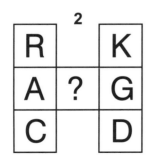
2

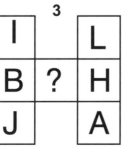
3

30

Can you complete these puzzles?

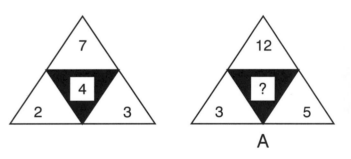

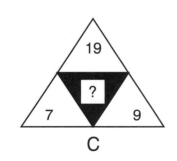
A

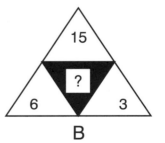
B   C

1

Which of the six numbered shapes goes in the empty square?

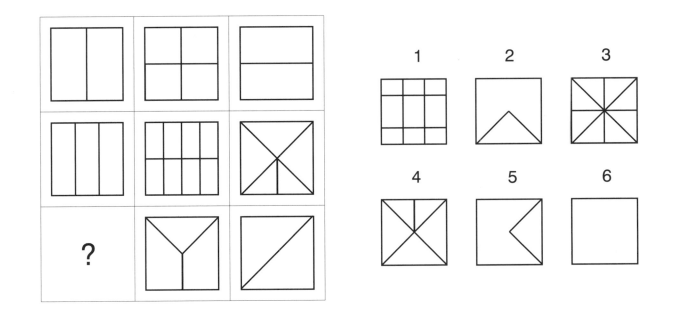

2

Which number finishes this sequence?

2
4
7
11
16
?

3

Can you fill in the blanks?

B J

E N

? ?

K V

N Z

Q D

LEVEL 4

4

Using the same rule for each box can you complete this teaser?

A

27	36	6
11	14	?

B

9	18	24
5	8	?

C

15	30	3
7	12	?

D

42	12	21
16	6	?

5

Which letter is the odd one out in each circle?

1

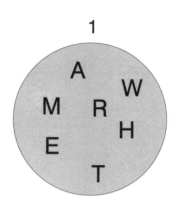

2

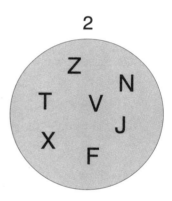

6

Can you fill in the blanks?

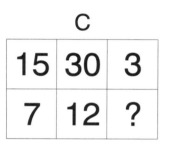

A

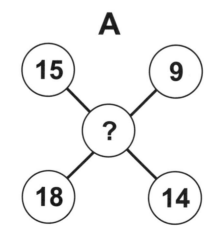

B

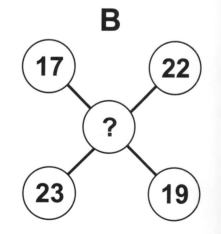

- 38 -

7

Can you insert the missing number?

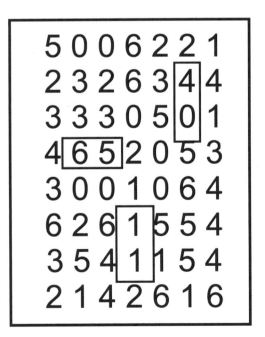

8

Using the numbers and symbols that appear in the top line in every row and column, can you complete this puzzle?

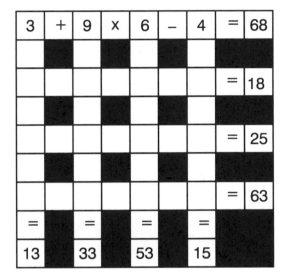

9

The numbers in the diagram represent a complete set of dominoes. The blank is represented by 0. Some dominoes are vertical, others are horizontal. Three dominoes have been highlighted for you but can you draw in the rest? You might find it easier using the checklist on the right.

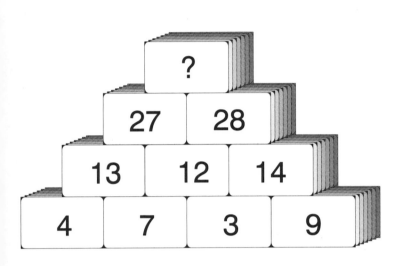

10

Which of these six watches should replace the blank one?

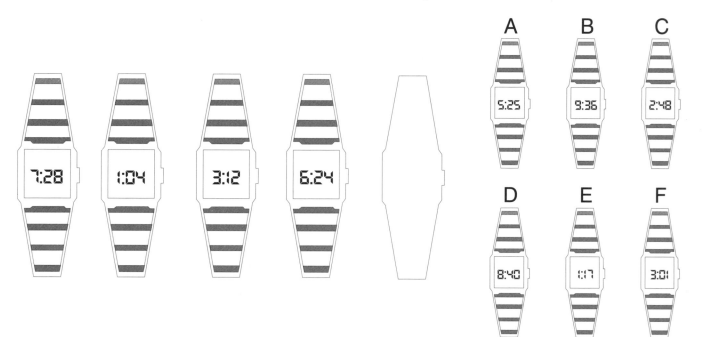

7:28   1:04   3:12   6:24

A — 5:25
B — 9:36
C — 2:48
D — 8:40
E — 1:17
F — 3:01

11

Can you fill in the blank?

A
F
P
E
Y
?
B

12

Continuing the logic used in the centre puzzle, can you work out which numbers are missing?

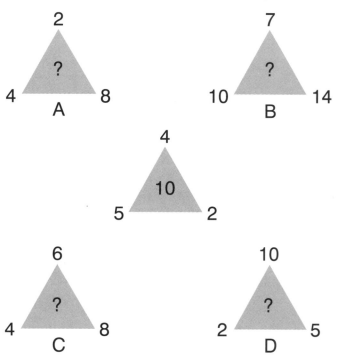

A: 2 (top), 4 (left), 8 (right), ? (centre)

B: 7 (top), 10 (left), 14 (right), ? (centre)

4 (top), 5 (left), 2 (right), 10 (centre)

C: 6 (top), 4 (left), 8 (right), ? (centre)

D: 10 (top), 2 (left), 5 (right), ? (centre)

13

Which of the five numbered pieces goes in the shaded area?

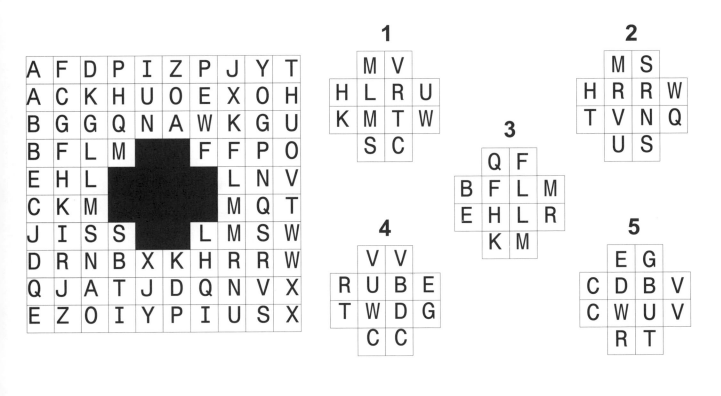

1

M	V	
H	L	R	U
K	M	T	W
S	C	

2

M	S	
H	R	R	W
T	V	N	Q
U	S	

3

Q	F	
B	F	L	M
E	H	L	R
K	M	

4

V	V	
R	U	B	E
T	W	D	G
C	C	

5

E	G	
C	D	B	V
C	W	U	V
R	T	

14

Solve this riddle

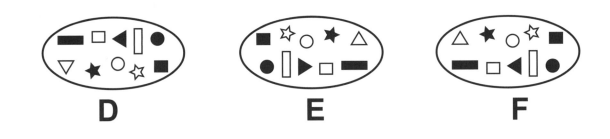

A   is to   **B**   as   **C**   is to

D   **E**   **F**

- 41 -

15

Can you move three circles and turn the pyramid upside down?

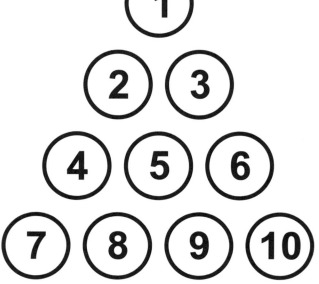

16

Why is this sum correct?

$$\begin{array}{r} 29 \\ -\ 1 \\ \hline 30 \end{array}$$

17

Finishing at the square with a star in it - can you find the start point in this grid?

Move one square North when you land on a square marked N1, two squares South when you land on a square marked S2 etc. etc.

5E	3S	1S	1S	2W	4S
1S	★	2W	4S	3W	3W
5E	1E	1S	1E	1N	1N
1S	1W	1E	1N	2S	1W
2E	2N	3N	1E	4N	4W
5N	3E	2W	1N	1E	2W

18

Draw three straight lines and separate the box into six sections, each one containing six fruits, two of each kind.

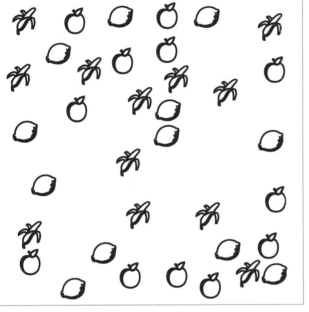

19

Each symbol represents a different number. Can you reconstruct the sum by replacing each symbol with a number?

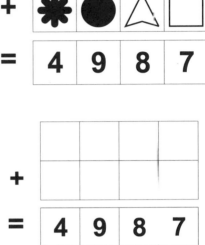

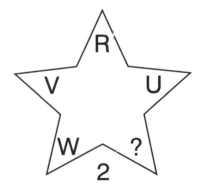

20

Can you work out which letters are missing?

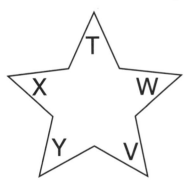

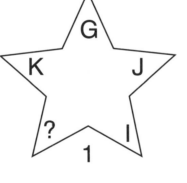

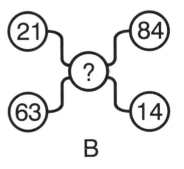

21

Can you work out which numbers are missing?

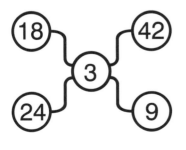

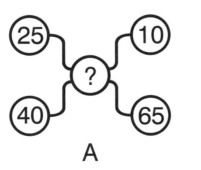

B

22

Which of the six numbered pieces will complete the sequence?

23

One of the following statements is incorrect - which one?

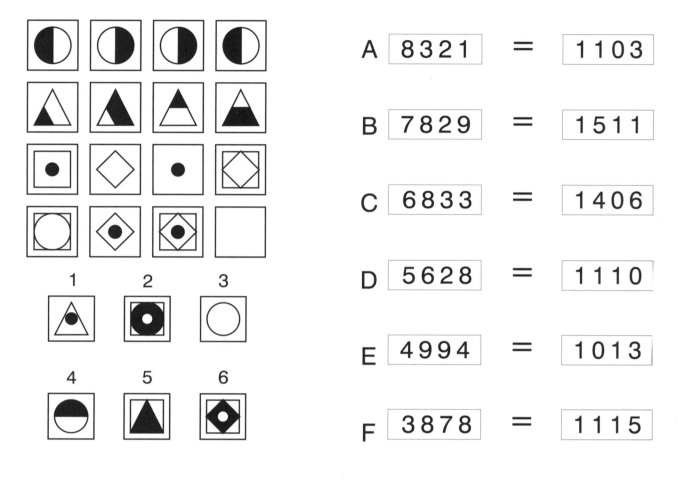

A 8321 = 1103

B 7829 = 1511

C 6833 = 1406

D 5628 = 1110

E 4994 = 1013

F 3878 = 1115

24

Can you work out what numbers are missing?

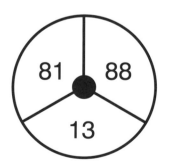

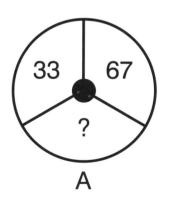

A

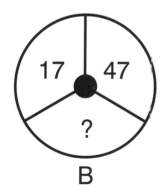

B

25

Can you insert the missing numbers?

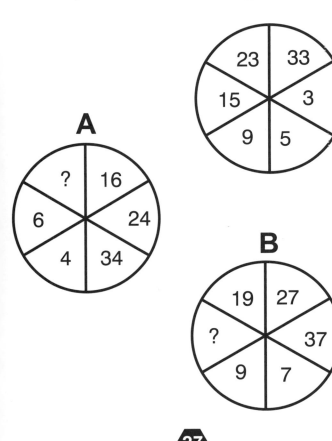

A

B

26

Which number is the odd one out in each group?

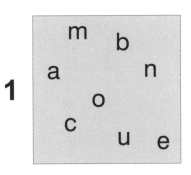

1

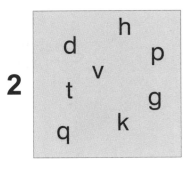

2

27

If a leaf is worth 6, can you work out what the other symbols are worth?

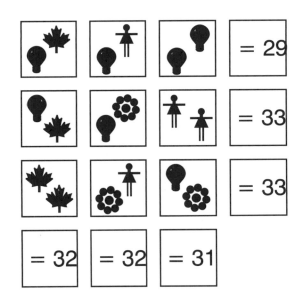

28

Every number between 1 and 16 should be put into this grid so that each row, column and diagonal adds up to the same total. Some numbers have already been added to give you a start.

13			16
	10	11	
	6		
1			4

1

Which of these five cubes can be made from the template?

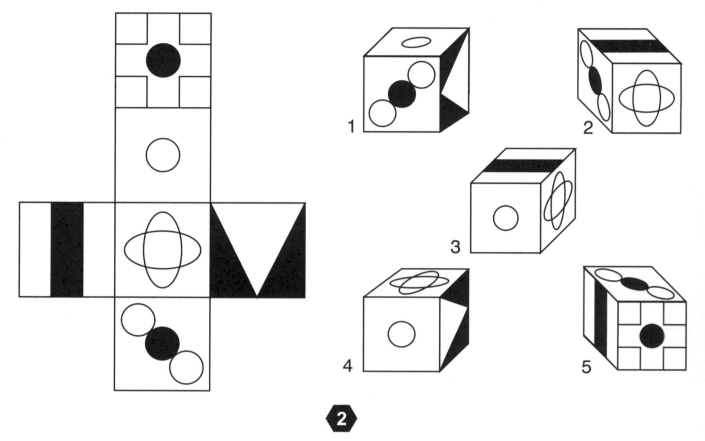

2

*Bill, who has a moustache identical to Bryan, is holding a clipboard.
He is wearing the same colour trousers as Barry, but not Bernie, and
the same colour hat as Bob. Can you work out who is who?*

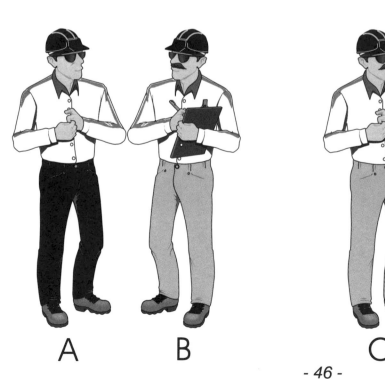

A   B   C   D   E

3

Can you fill in the blanks?

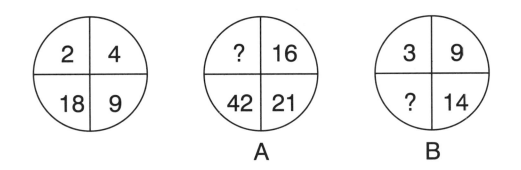

A   B

4

Which letter is missing?

5

Can you replace the question mark?

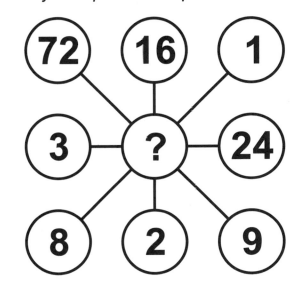

6

Can you fill in the blanks?

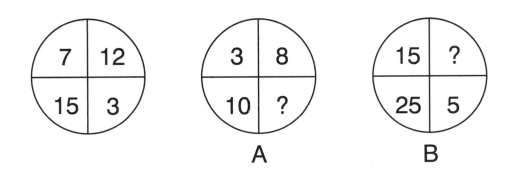

A   B

7

What is the value of each shape?

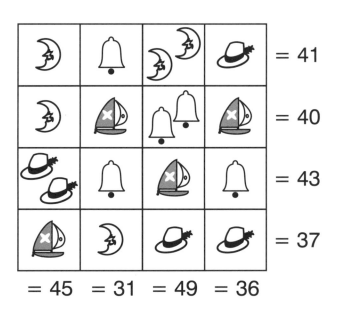

= 45   = 31   = 49   = 36

8

Insert the numbers 1 - 9 inclusive into the number trail to reach the answer.

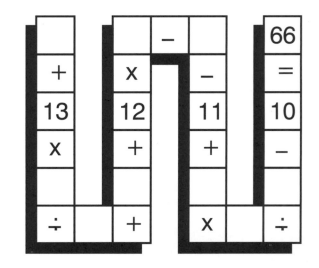

9

Mr Jones, the local baker, was aked how many loaves of bread he had sold last Monday. Feeling rather mischievious he said:

"My first customer bought half of my bread plus half a loaf extra. My second customer, Mrs Smith, bought half of what was left plus half a loaf more. The third customer asked for half of what I had left plus an extra half a loaf to feed the ducks at the local park."

By the time Mr Black, the fourth customer, visited the shop he had sold out of all his bread. He did not sell any half loaves. Can you work out how many loaves he sold?

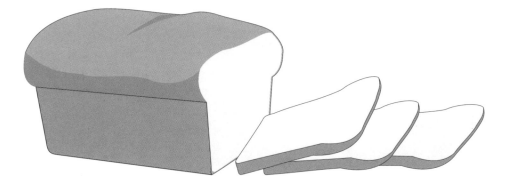

10

Which letter completes the sequence?

11

Add the correct number to the empty box.

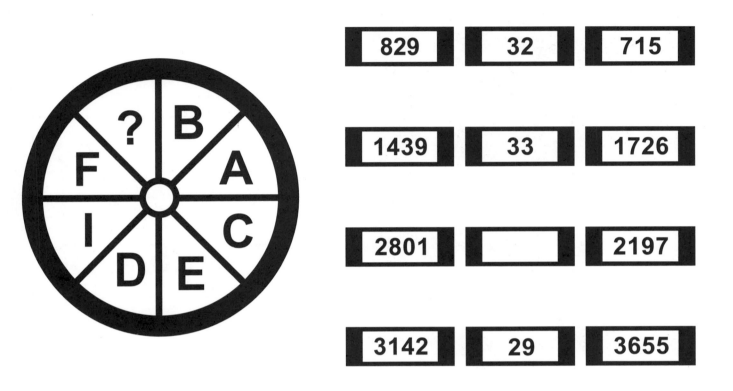

829	32	715
1439	33	1726
2801		2197
3142	29	3655

12

Which shape continues this sequence?

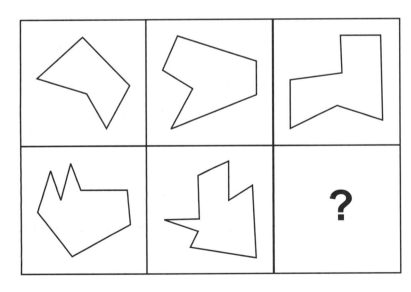

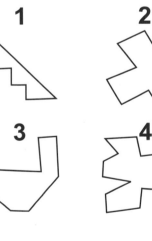

1
2
3
4
5
6

13

Peter Penguin and his friends have fallen out with each other. Can you get them back to their homes without crossing paths?

14

Can you work out which number is missing?

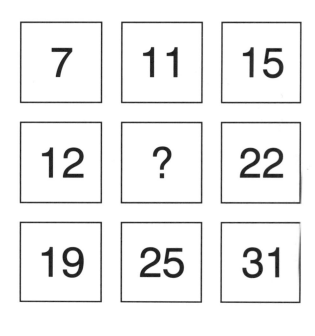

7	11	15
12	?	22
19	25	31

15

Every number between 0 and 9 inclusive has been used in this sum. Unfortunately some have been replaced by letters. Can you work out which number replaces each letter?

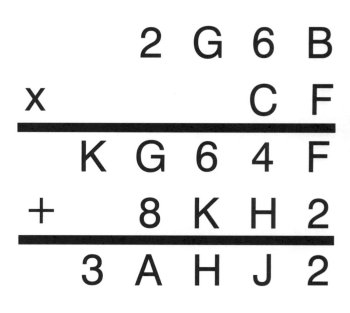

```
      2 G 6 B
  X       C F
  _____
    K G 6 4 F
  +   8 K H 2
  _____
    3 A H J 2
```

16

Can you fill in the blanks?

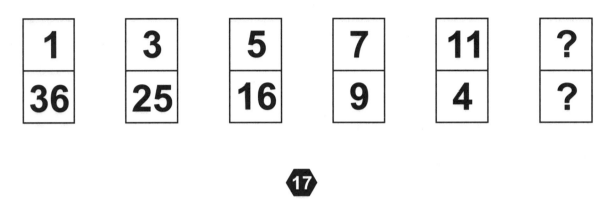

17

Which square continues the sequence?

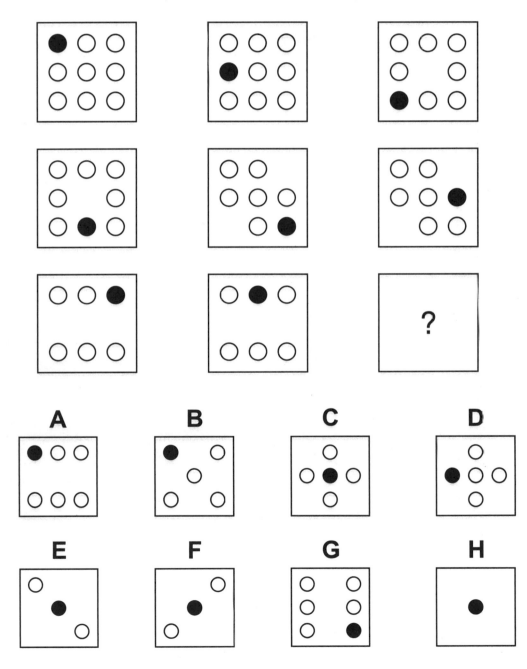

18

Can you replace the question mark?

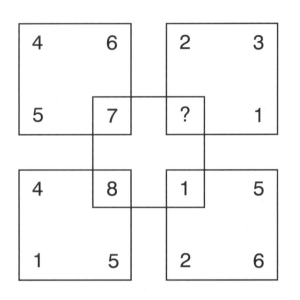

19

Can you find the missing numbers?

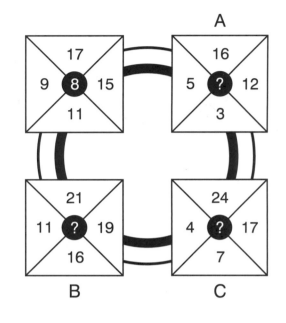

20

Can you work out who is married to whom?

21

Which box continues the sequence?

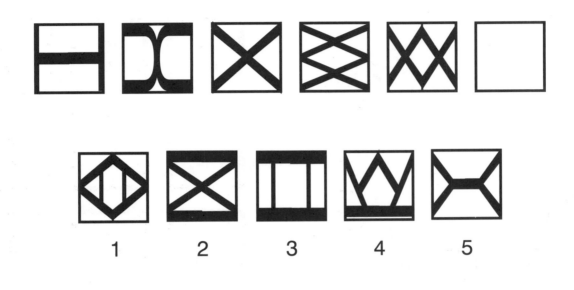

1   2   3   4   5

22

Which letter replaces the blank and completes the sequence?

23

Can you replace the missing number?

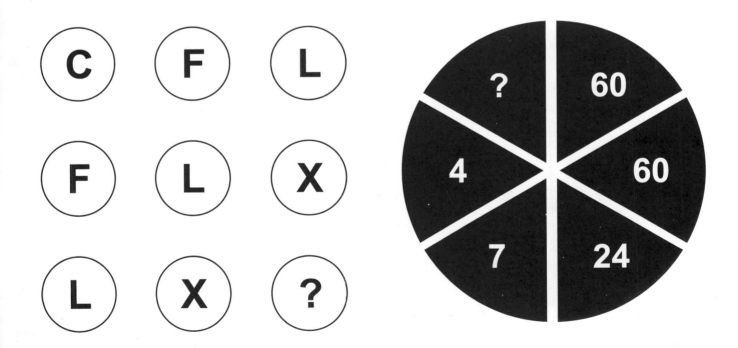

24

What letter replaces the blank and completes the chain?

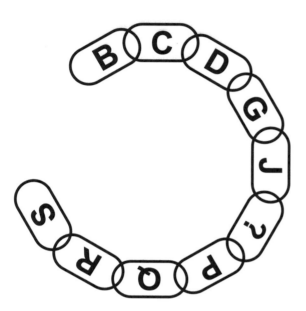

25

Can you replace the missing number?

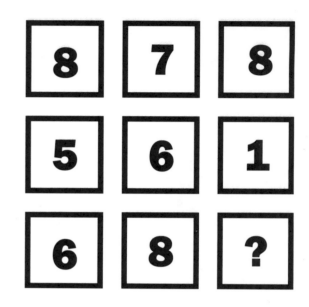

8	7	8
5	6	1
6	8	?

26

Which letters replace the blanks?

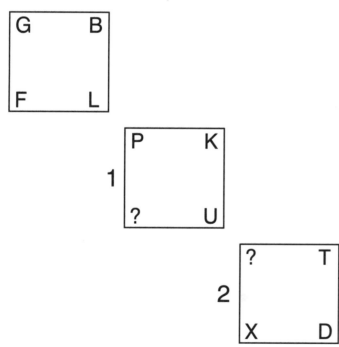

G	B
F	L

1
P	K
?	U

2
?	T
X	D

27

Can you complete the sequence?

60

57

54

51

50

?

1

Can you fill in the missing numbers?

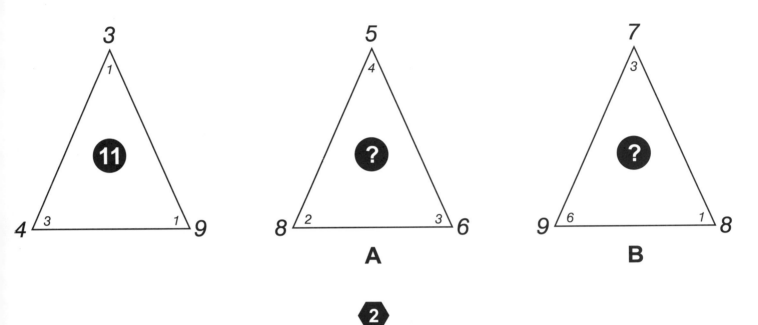

3
1
11
4 3   1 9

5
4
?
8 2   3 6
A

7
3
?
9 6   1 8
B

2

Can you work out which letters are missing from each line?

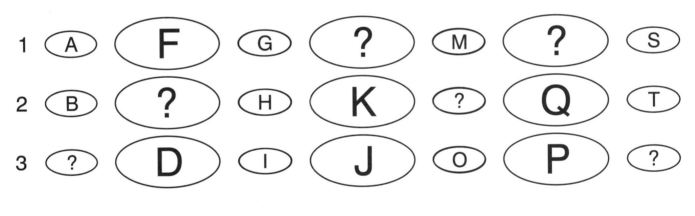

1 A F G ? M ? S

2 B ? H K ? Q T

3 ? D I J O P ?

3

Can you replace the missing numbers?

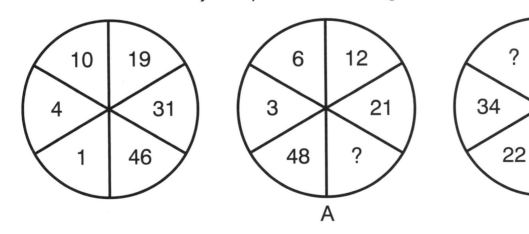

10	19
4	31
1	46

6	12
3	21
48	?
A

?	4
34	7
22	13
B

4

Six college students all share the same flat. Last Monday morning one of the girls, Hannah, was trying to do her maths homework when she realised that her friends might be able to help her. "Can you do me a favour" she asked the three boys? I would like you to each eat three pieces of toast with jam on, three pieces with honey on and three pieces with marmalade."
The boys readily agreed to this task and made for the toaster straight away.
Hannah then turned to the girls, " I would like each of you to eat two pieces of toast with butter on and two pieces with honey on."
"That sounds easy," said Helen, the oldest of the group.
"Yes," replied Hannah, "but there is a catch."

When everybody gathered around together she laid out the rules:

"Nobody can eat toast that they have made themselves.
Harry must eat the toast that Helen has made.
Henry must not eat the toast that Heidi has made.
Howard must only eat toast that has been made by Harry.
You must all make me one piece of toast with jam."

How many pieces of toast did the girls put in the toaster?

5

Move one of the lines that make up the numbers to make this sum correct.

93÷27−30÷16 = 68

6

Put these ten pears around the table so that there is an equal number on each edge.

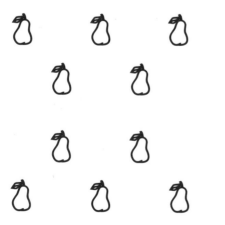

- 56 -

7

Which number is missing?

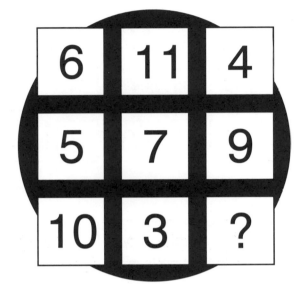

8

Which letter is missing?

9

Work out the logic and fill in the missing number.

10

Can you replace the missing letters?

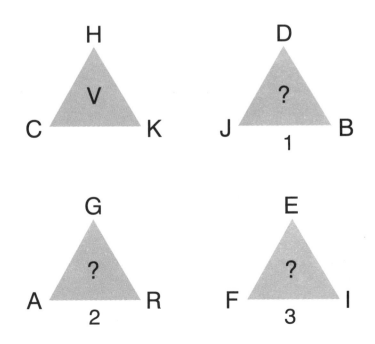

11

Can you fill in the blanks - sorry no example this time!

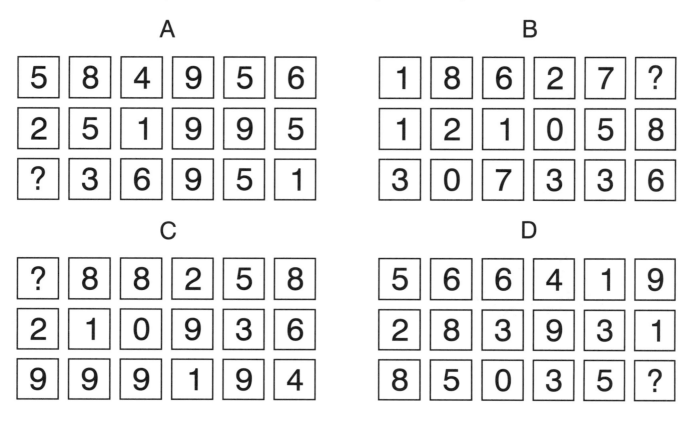

A

5	8	4	9	5	6
2	5	1	9	9	5
?	3	6	9	5	1

B

1	8	6	2	7	?
1	2	1	0	5	8
3	0	7	3	3	6

C

?	8	8	2	5	8
2	1	0	9	3	6
9	9	9	1	9	4

D

5	6	6	4	1	9
2	8	3	9	3	1
8	5	0	3	5	?

12

Which hexagon continues the sequence?

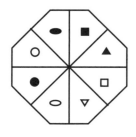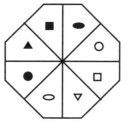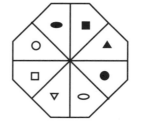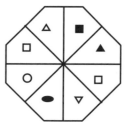

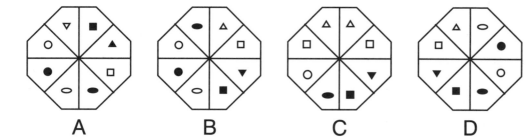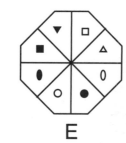

13

Which card replaces the blank one?

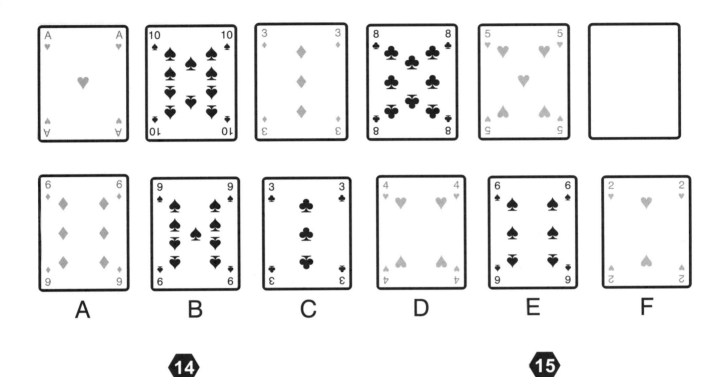

A   B   C   D   E   F

14

Every number between 1 and 25 should go into this grid so that each row, column and diagonal adds up to 65.

21		15		
				20
		13		
10				
25				5

15

Add one of each of these symbols to every box so that no row, column or diagonal of any length contains more than one of each symbol.

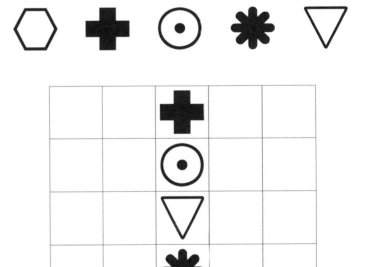

16

Which of these shapes is the odd one out?

1

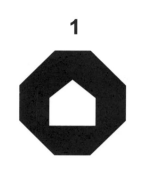

2

3

4

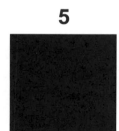

5

6

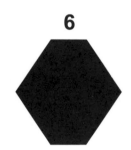

7

8

9

10

17

Complete these puzzles.

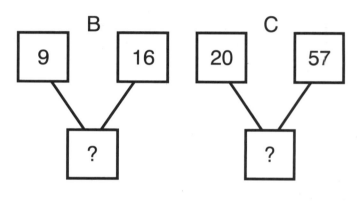

A

| 17 | 23 | 32 | 41 |

| 13 | ? |

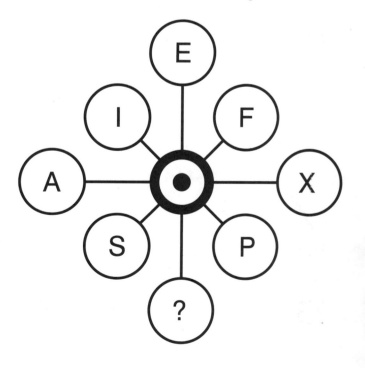

B   C

| 9 | 16 | 20 | 57 |

| ? | ? |

18

Which letter is missing?

E I F A X S P ?

19

Can you replace the missing letters?

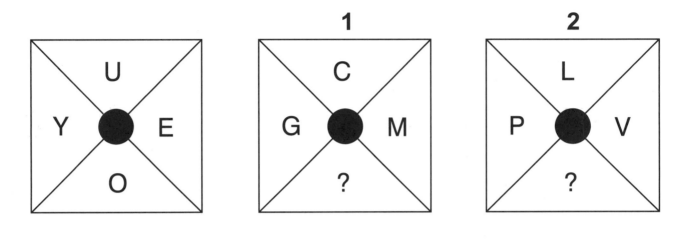

20

Can you work out the logic and solve this puzzle?

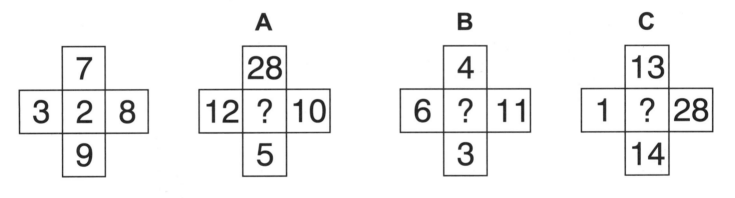

21

Which number replaces the blank?

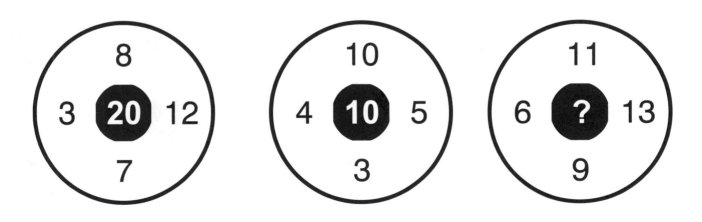

22

Using eight of these pieces can you return this word domino puzzle back to its original form?

T	Q		V	Y		H	J		J	V
E	N		A	Y		T	A		A	A
A	R		J	Y		A	V		T	P

P	A	Z		Z			C
		B					A
Z	B						
T	H	A	X	D	M	
Q			D	O	E	
C			M			

23

Which number is missing?

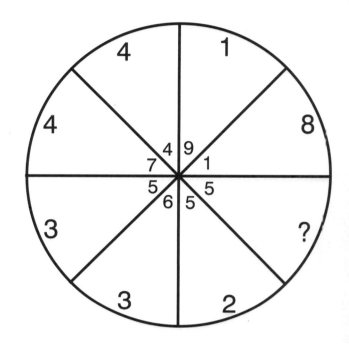

24

1

2

Phillip has the same plant as Paul and the same shorts as Peter. He has also got a white shirt. Patrick's shirt is grey but Percy's is not.

Can you work out who is who?

3

4

5

25

What is the value of the third row?

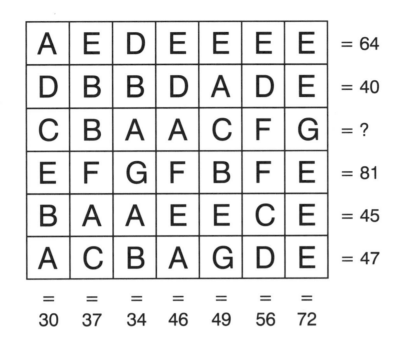

A	E	D	E	E	E	E	= 64
D	B	B	D	A	D	E	= 40
C	B	A	A	C	F	G	= ?
E	F	G	F	B	F	E	= 81
B	A	A	E	E	C	E	= 45
A	C	B	A	G	D	E	= 47

= 30 = 37 = 34 = 46 = 49 = 56 = 72

26

Which square replaces the empty one?

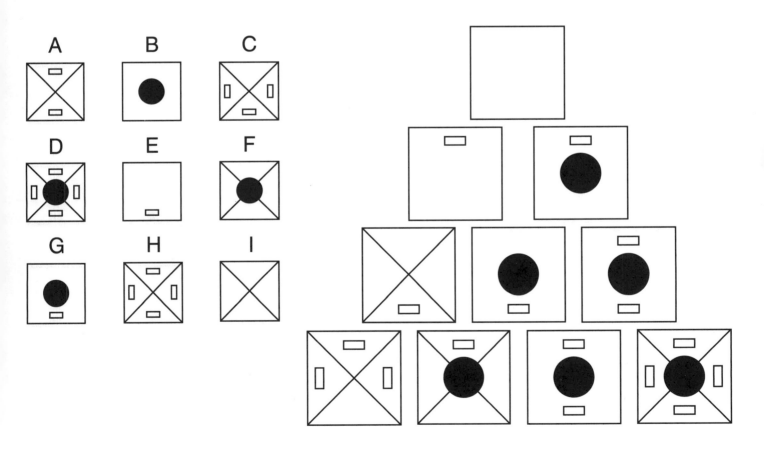

A B C

D E F

G H I

27

What time should the blank clock show?

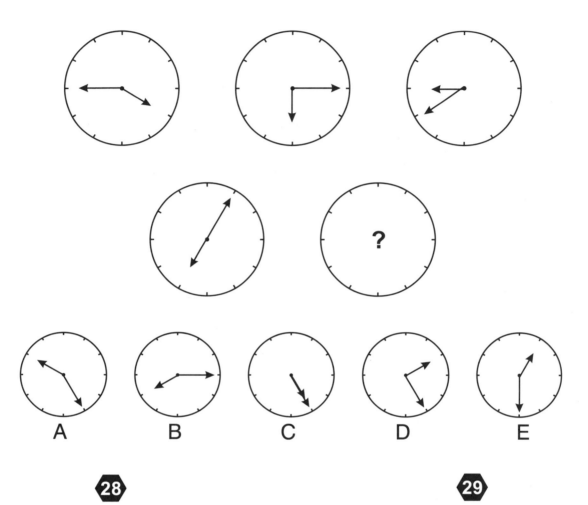

A   B   C   D   E

28

Farmer Giles had 5 black cows, 3 brown, 4 brown and white, 6 black and white and 7 black and brown ones.

How many of these cows could say they had markings at least fifty percent similar to the rest of the herd?

29

Can you complete these puzzles?

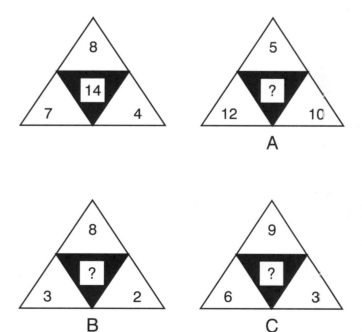

A

B

C

1

Which of the six numbered stars goes in the empty square?

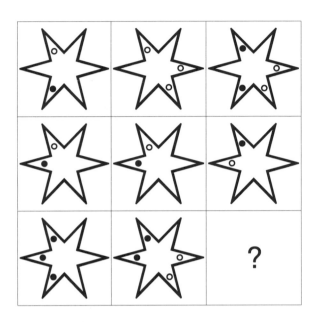

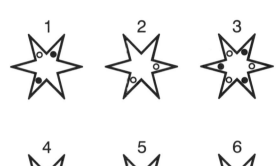

2

Which letter is two down from the letter three up from the letter two down from the letter three up from the last letter?

3

Which number replaces the blank?

5	8	12
7	3	9
11	10	?

4

Using the same rule for each box can you complete this teaser?

5

Which letter is the odd one out in each circle?

A

3	9	3
5	7	?

B

2	6	2
9	19	?

1

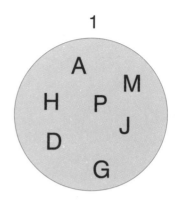

C

8	12	2
13	15	?

D

15	31	8
6	18	?

2

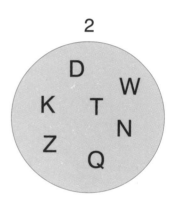

6

Can you fill in the blanks?

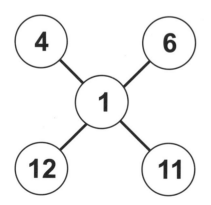

A

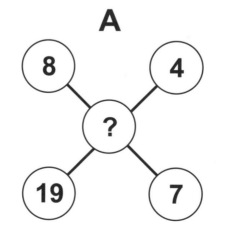

B

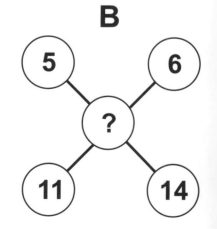

7

Can you insert the missing number?

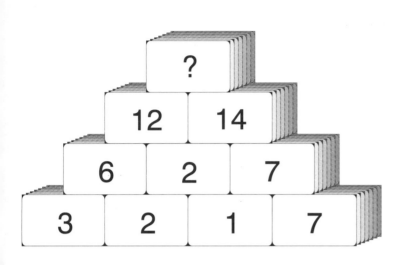

8

Using the numbers and symbols that appear in the top line in every row and column, can you complete this puzzle?

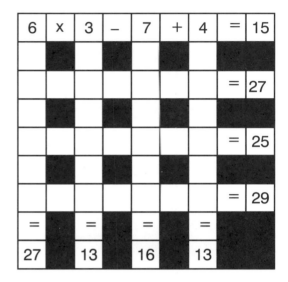

6	x	3	–	7	+	4	=	15
							=	27
							=	25
							=	29
=		=		=		=		
27		13		16		13		

9

The numbers in the diagram represent a complete set of dominoes. The blank is represented by 0. Some dominoes are vertical, others are horizontal. Two dominoes have been highlighted for you but can you draw in the rest? You might find it easier using the checklist on the right.

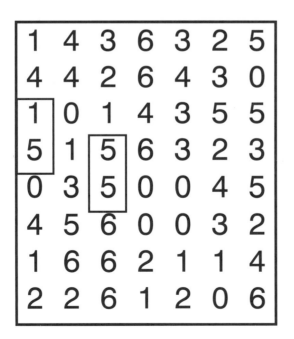

1	4	3	6	3	2	5
4	4	2	6	4	3	0
1	0	1	4	3	5	5
5	1	5	6	3	2	3
0	3	5	0	0	4	5
4	5	6	0	0	3	2
1	6	6	2	1	1	4
2	2	6	1	2	0	6

0 0		2 3	
0 1		2 4	
0 2		2 5	
0 3		2 6	
0 4		3 3	
0 5		3 4	
0 6		3 5	
1 1		3 6	
1 2		4 4	
1 3		4 5	
1 4		4 6	
1 5	✓	5 5	✓
1 6		5 6	
2 2		6 6	

10

Which of these six watches should replace the blank one?

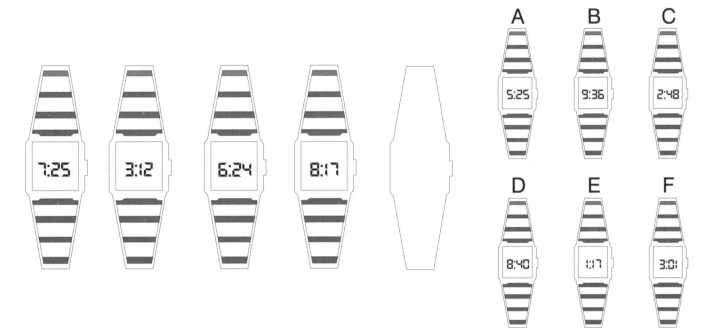

A   B   C

5:25   9:36   2:48

D   E   F

8:40   1:17   3:01

11

Can you fill in the blank?

B

L

G

?

L

V

Q

12

Continuing the logic used in the first puzzle, can you work out what the missing numbers are?

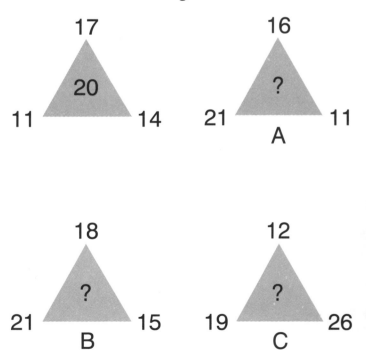

17
20
11   14

16
?
21   11
A

18
?
21   15
B

12
?
19   26
C

13

Which of the five numbered pieces goes in the shaded area?

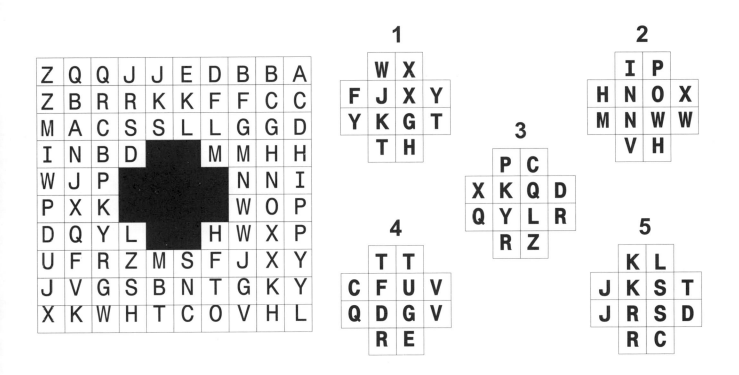

14

Claire and her friends took part in a chess competition last weekend. From the information given can you work out their names and their final positions?

15

Which cube can be made from this shape?

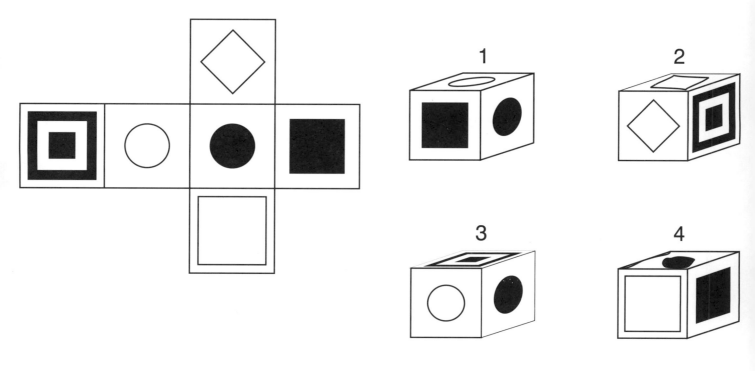

16

Every number between 1 and 25 should go into this grid so that each row, column and diagonal adds up to 65.

17		1		
				16
		13		
10				
11				9

17

Add one of each of these symbols to every box so that no row, column or diagonal of any length contains more than one of each symbol.

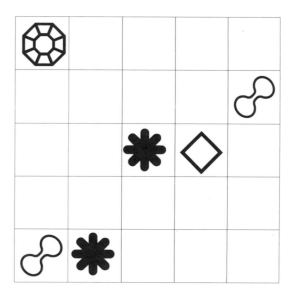

18

Can you work out which letter is missing?

19

Work out the logic and fill in the missing number.

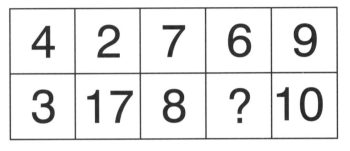

20

Can you work out which letters are missing?

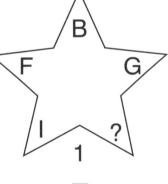

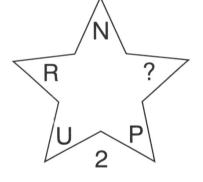

21

Can you work out which numbers are missing?

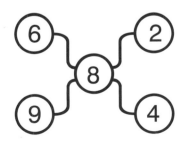

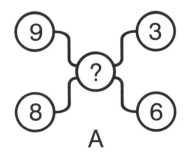

A

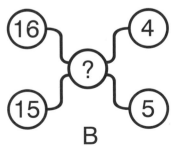

B

22

Which of the six numbered pieces will complete the sequence?

23

One of the following statements is incorrect - which one?

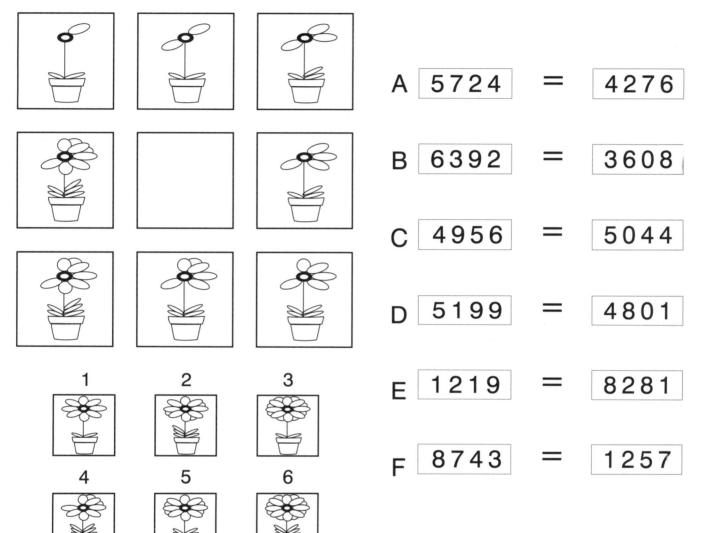

A | 5724 | = | 4276

B | 6392 | = | 3608

C | 4956 | = | 5044

D | 5199 | = | 4801

E | 1219 | = | 8281

F | 8743 | = | 1257

24

Can you work out which numbers are missing?

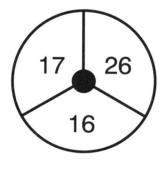

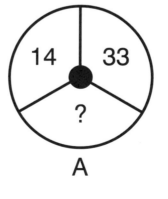

A

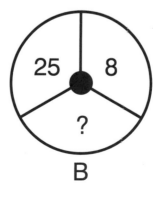

B

25

Can you insert the missing numbers?

A

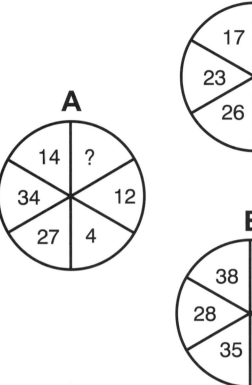

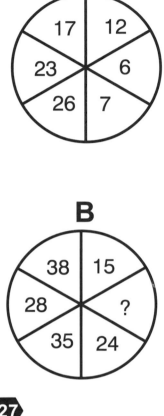

B

26

Which number is the odd one out in each group?

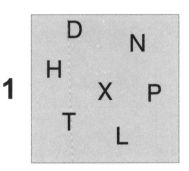

1

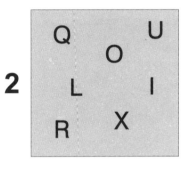

2

27

John, Joe and Jamie were out collecting money for charity last week. John collected three times as much as Jamie, Joe collected twice as much as John.

If the total amount collected was £900, can you work out how much each person collected?

28

Every number between 9 and 17 should be put into this grid so that each row, column and diagonal adds up to the same total. Some numbers have already been added to give you a start.

	11	
14		

1

Only two cubes can be made from this shape - Can you work out which ones?

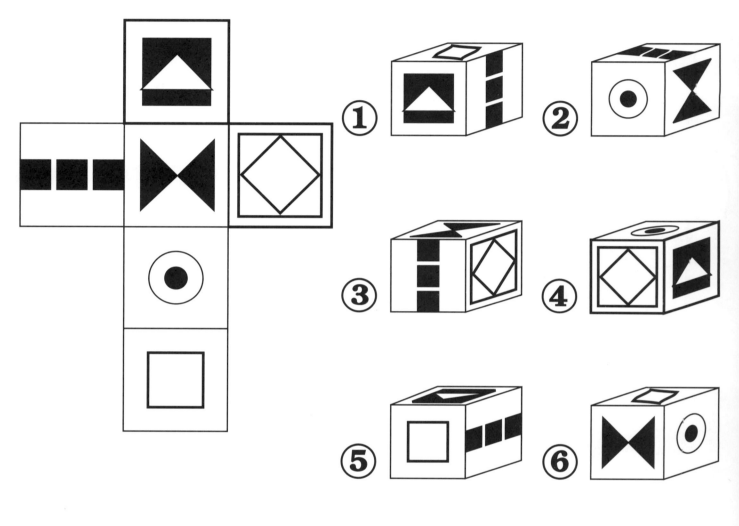

2

Insert one of each symbol in each sum.

$$\boxed{-} \quad \boxed{\div} \quad \boxed{X} \quad \boxed{+}$$

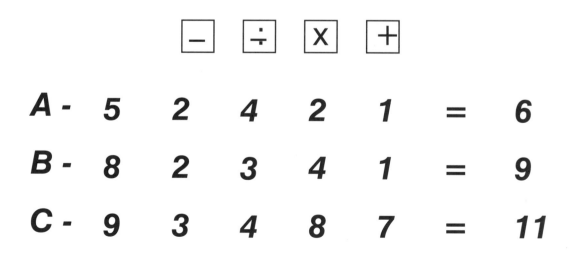

A - 5   2   4   2   1   =   6

B - 8   2   3   4   1   =   9

C - 9   3   4   8   7   =   11

3

Work out the logic and complete the puzzle.

D	H
S	W

G	C
X	T

B	J
Q	Y

L	E
?	O

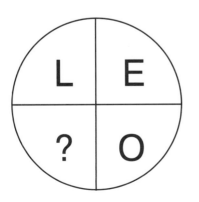

4

Which number is missing?

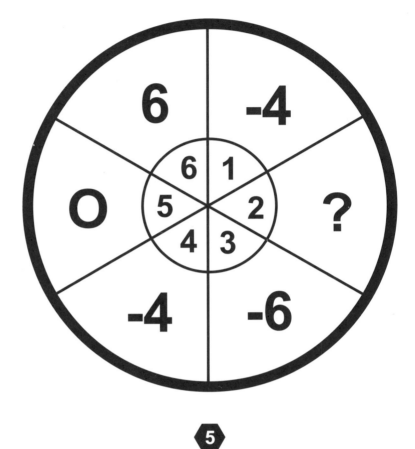

5

Can you replace the question mark?

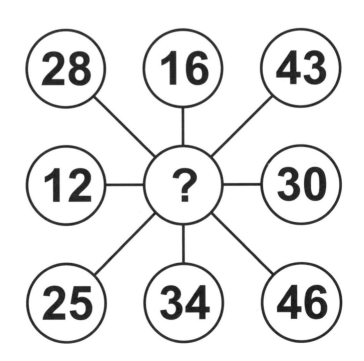

6

Which number is missing?

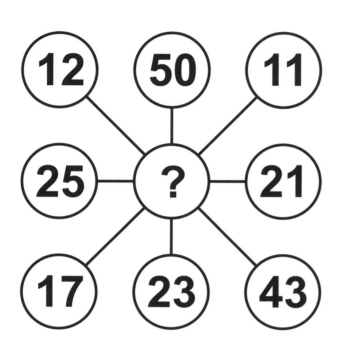

7

Can you work out the logic
and solve the puzzle?

8

Can you work out which number is missing?

9

Complete the puzzle.

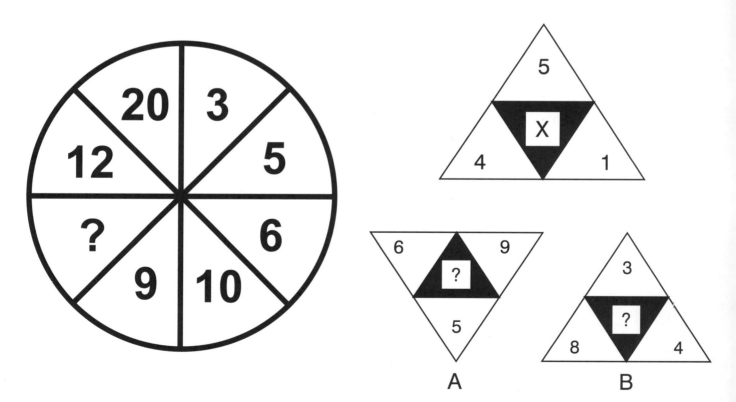

Which letter is the odd one out?

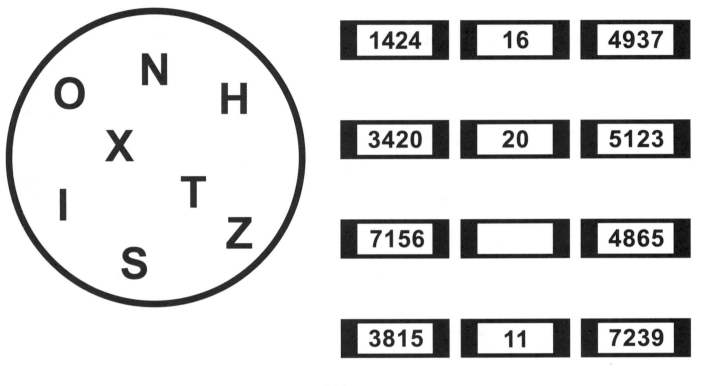

11

Add the correct number to the empty box.

1424	16	4937
3420	20	5123
7156		4865
3815	11	7239

12

Which shape continues this sequence?

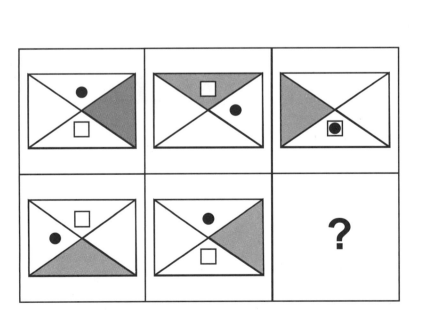

1

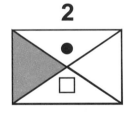

2

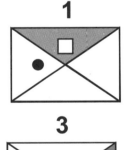

3

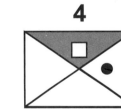

5

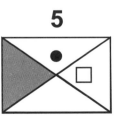

6

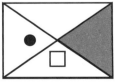

Which square is the odd one out?

1
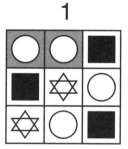

2
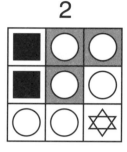

3
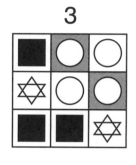

4
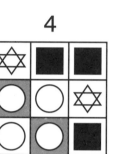

5
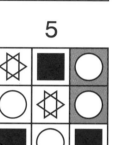

6
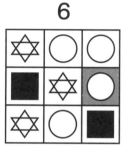

7
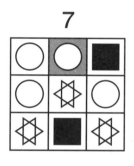

8
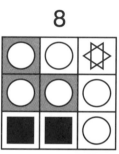

9
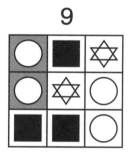

Which number is missing?

2	7	3	2
4	1	?	4
7	3	2	2
1	3	4	8

Insert the numbers 2 - 9 into this grid so that every row adds up to 18.

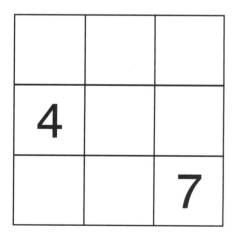

16

Can you fill in the blanks?

  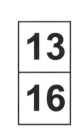 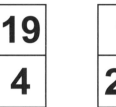 

7	25	13	?	19	1
36	11	16	?	4	23

17

Which square goes in the centre?

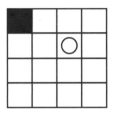 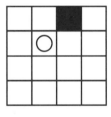 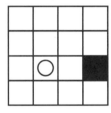

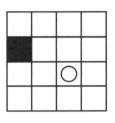 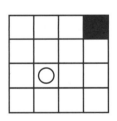 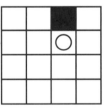

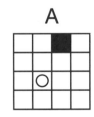 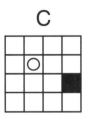

A   B   C

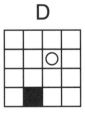 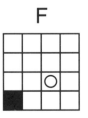

D   E   F

18

Can you replace the question mark?

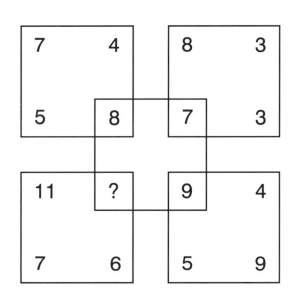

19

Can you find the missing numbers?

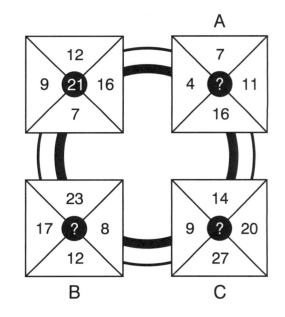

20

Which letter is missing?

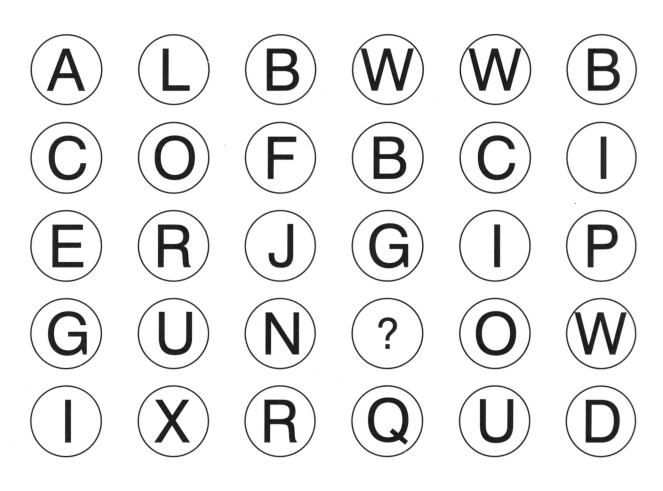

21

Which number completes this puzzle?

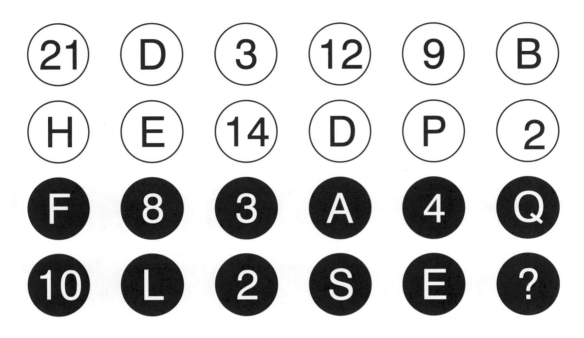

22

Which letter replaces the blank and completes the sequence?

23

Which numbers replace the blanks?

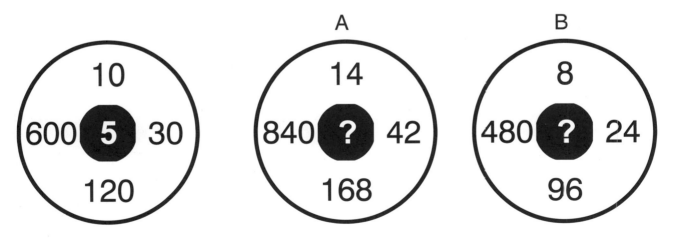

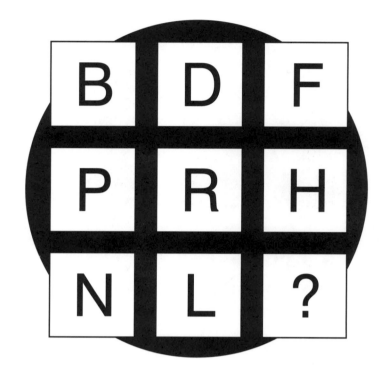

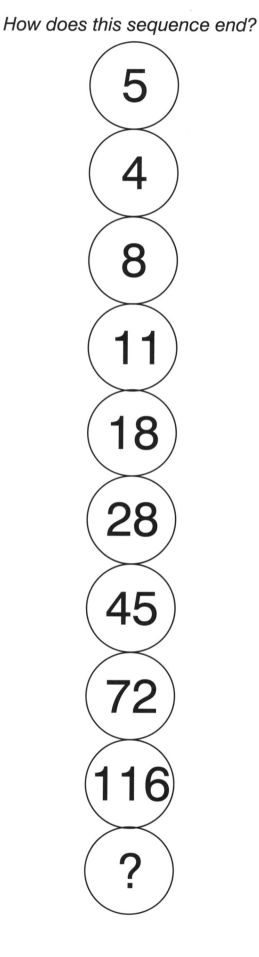

24

How does this sequence end?

5
4
8
11
18
28
45
72
116
?

25

Can you insert the missing letter?

B	D	F
P	R	H
N	L	?

26

Work out the logic and replace the missing letters.

P	D		R	
	A	Z		E
K		U		C
	Y	B	J	
S			T	H

27

Can you replace the question mark?

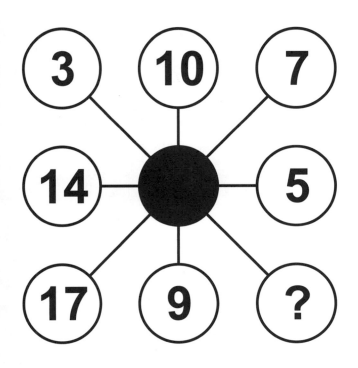

28

Which numbers are missing?

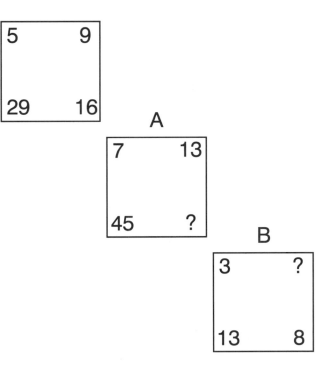

29

Which letter replaces the blank and completes the chain?

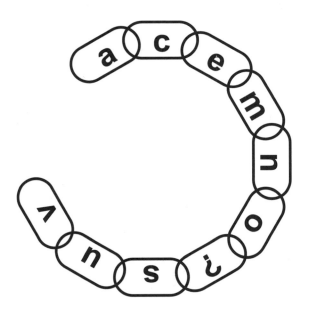

30

Can you replace the missing number?

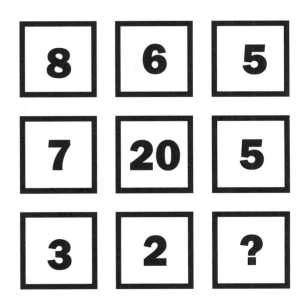

1

Can you insert the missing numbers?
(A different rule applies to each box.)

A

20	32	18
13	19	?

B

15	13	19
25	21	?

C

7	12	14
19	34	?

2

Which letter is the odd one out
in each circle?

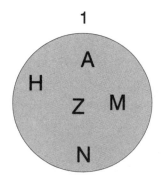

1

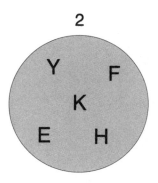

2

3

Can you fill in the blanks?

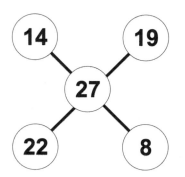

A

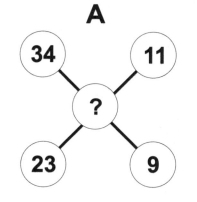

B

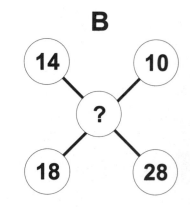

4

Which of these six watches should replace the blank one?

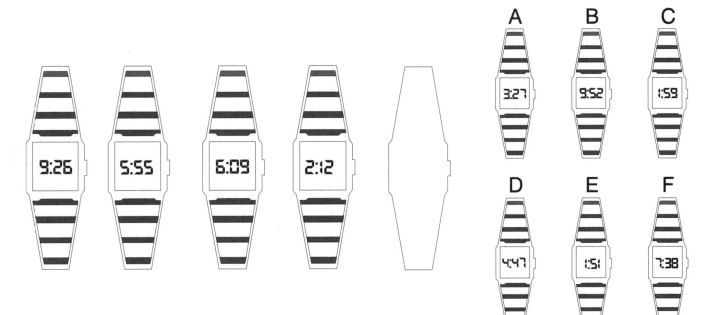

9:26 5:55 6:09 2:12

A 3:27 B 9:52 C 1:59
D 4:47 E 1:51 F 7:38

5

Can you fill in the blank?

B
D
G
J
?
Q
R

6

Can you work out the logic behind this puzzle?

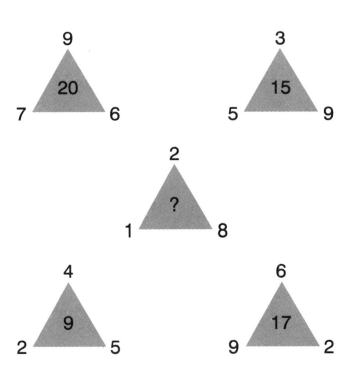

9
20
7   6

3
15
5   9

2
?
1   8

4
9
2   5

6
17
9   2

7

*By following the same rule as used in each of the
first three circles, can you complete the others?*

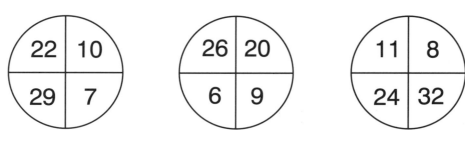

22	10
29	7

26	20
6	9

11	8
24	32

A

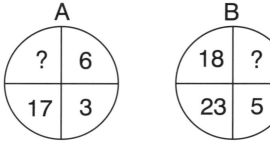

?	6
17	3

B

18	?
23	5

8

Which letter is missing?

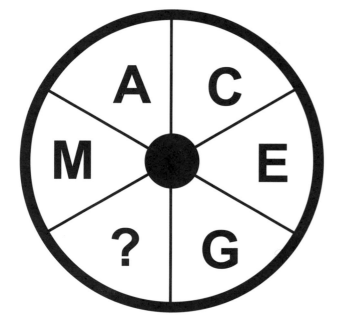

9

Can you replace the question mark?

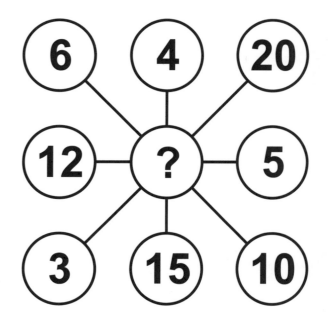

Which number is missing?

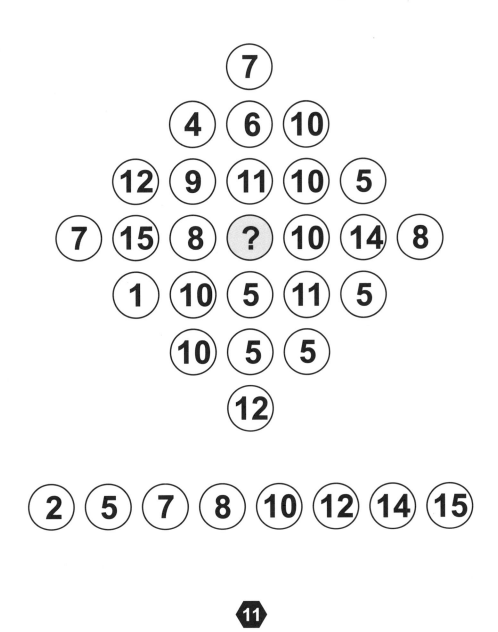

11

Can you work out which letter should replace the blank?

H   I   N   ?   S   X   Z

Can you work out which cards are missing from each row?

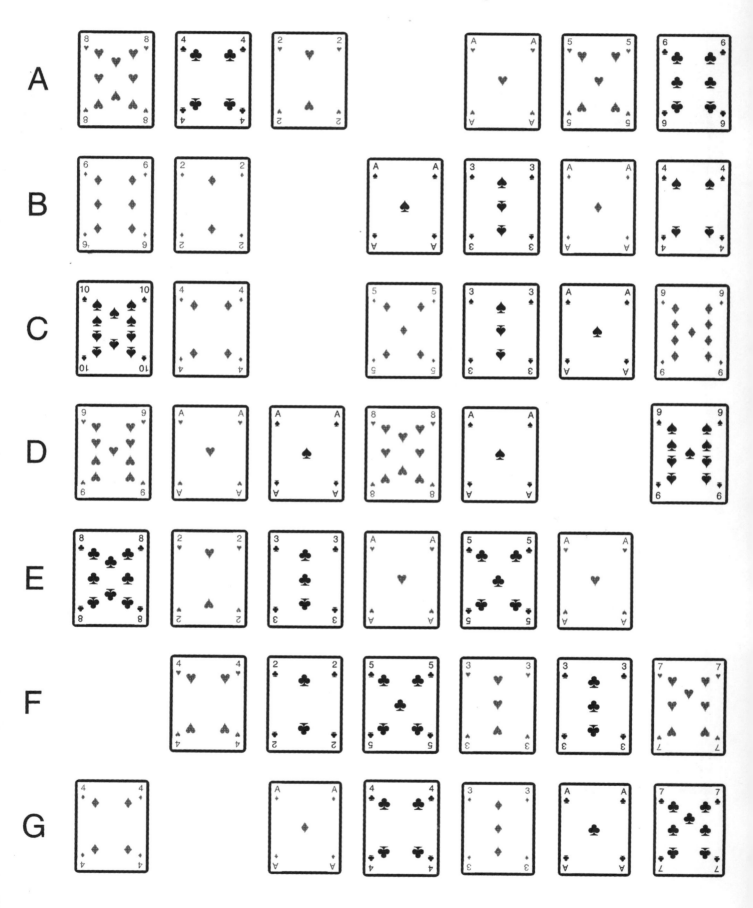

13

Which letter replaces the blank and completes the sequence?

H
S

K
P

Q
J

V
?

14

Can you complete this number square?

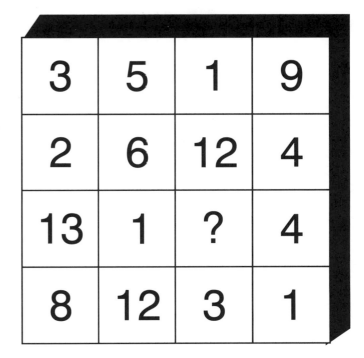

3	5	1	9
2	6	12	4
13	1	?	4
8	12	3	1

15

Can you fill in the blanks?

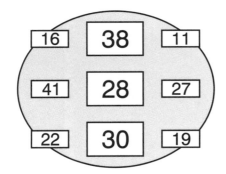

16	38	11
41	28	27
22	30	19

A

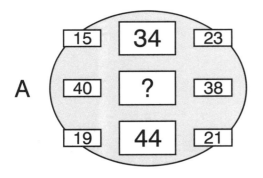

15	34	23
40	?	38
19	44	21

B

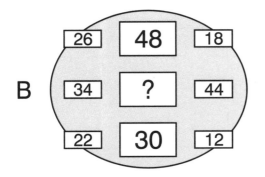

26	48	18
34	?	44
22	30	12

16

Study the example puzzles and, by using the same rule, can you complete the last puzzle?

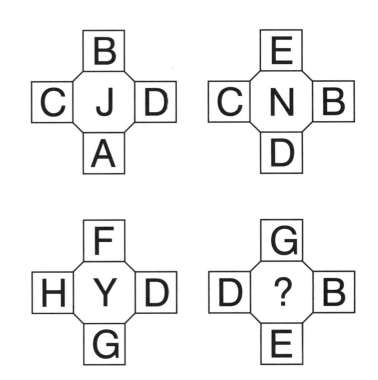

B
C J D
A

E
C N B
D

F
H Y D
G

G
D ? B
E

Which square completes the sequence?

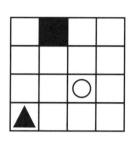 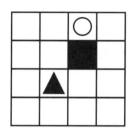 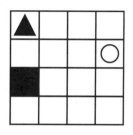

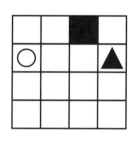 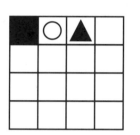 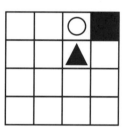

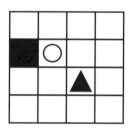 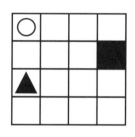 

A   B   C

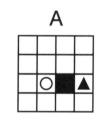 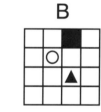 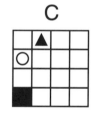

D   E   F

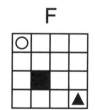

18

Hilary has only 3 children. She told her colleagues that half of her children are girls but she is not lying.

Can you explain?

19

Replace all the numbers so that each row and column adds up to 25

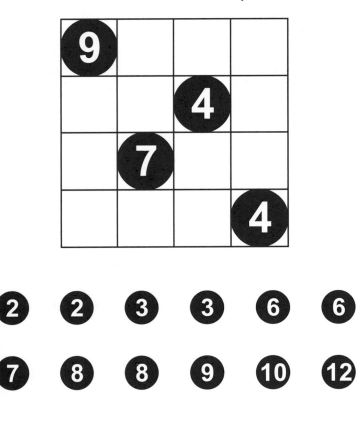

20

What does F equal?

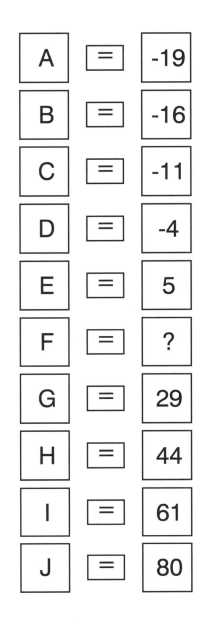

A	=	-19
B	=	-16
C	=	-11
D	=	-4
E	=	5
F	=	?
G	=	29
H	=	44
I	=	61
J	=	80

21

Which letter is missing?

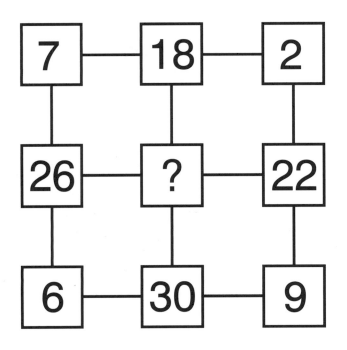

22

One, and only one, of these answers is incorrect - which one?

A - 4 + 3 + 5 = 8

B - 9 + 11 + 2 = 8

C - 8 + 4 + 12 = 8

D - 19 + 5 + 1 = 8

23

Can you complete these puzzles using the example given?

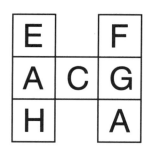
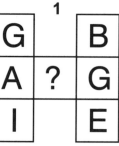

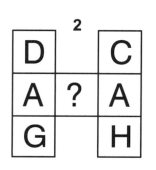

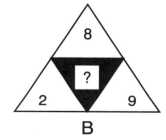

24

Can you complete these puzzles?

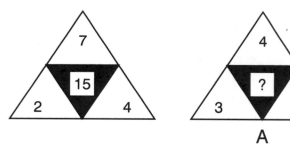

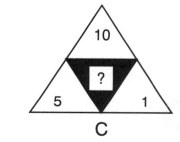

25

Can you work out what the missing letters are?

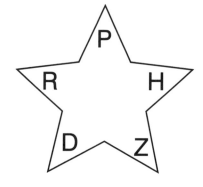
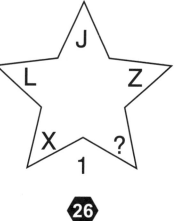
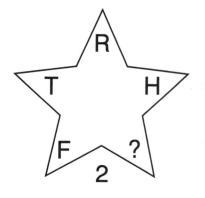

26

Can you work out what the missing numbers are?

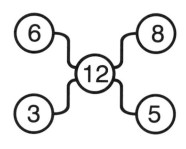
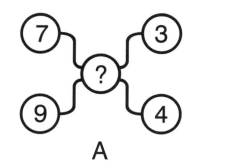
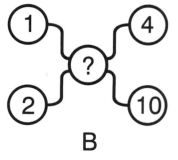

27

Can you fill in the missing numbers?

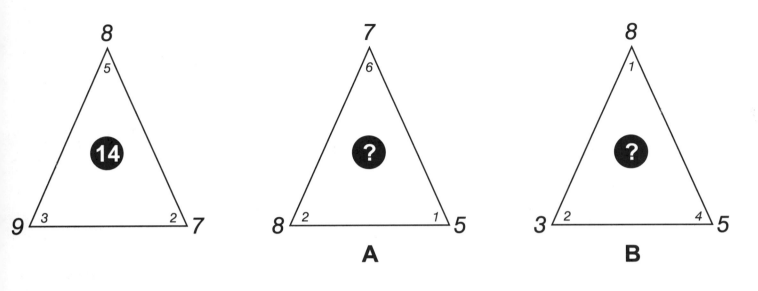

A　　　B

28

Can you work out which letters are missing from each line?

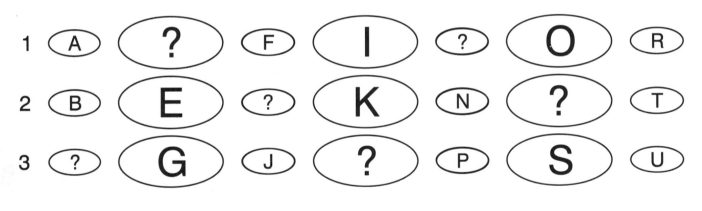

1　A　?　F　I　?　O　R

2　B　E　?　K　N　?　T

3　?　G　J　?　P　S　U

29

Can you complete these puzzles?

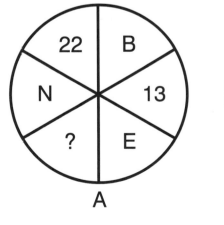

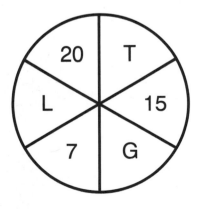

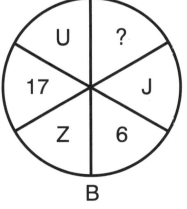

A　　　B

1

Which of the five numbered pieces goes in the shaded area?

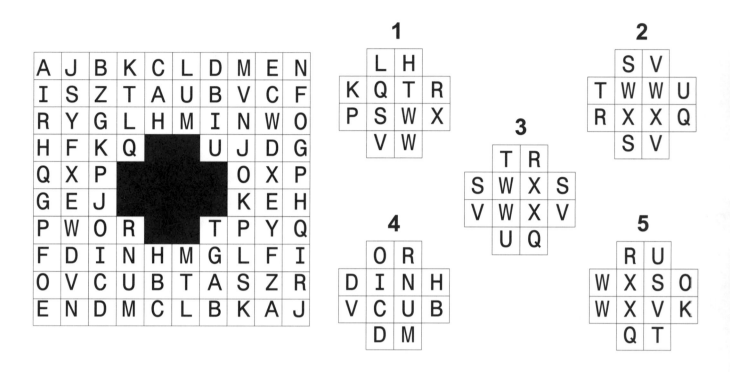

A	J	B	K	C	L	D	M	E	N
I	S	Z	T	A	U	B	V	C	F
R	Y	G	L	H	M	I	N	W	O
H	F	K	Q	■	■	U	J	D	G
Q	X	P	■	■	■	O	X	P	
G	E	J	■	■	■	K	E	H	
P	W	O	R	■	T	P	Y	Q	
F	D	I	N	H	M	G	L	F	I
O	V	C	U	B	T	A	S	Z	R
E	N	D	M	C	L	B	K	A	J

1

L	H		
K	Q	T	R
P	S	W	X
V	W		

2

	S	V	
T	W	W	U
R	X	X	Q
	S	V	

3

	T	R	
S	W	X	S
V	W	X	V
	U	Q	

4

	O	R	
D	I	N	H
V	C	U	B
	D	M	

5

	R	U	
W	X	S	O
W	X	V	K
	Q	T	

2

Which number completes this sequence?

3

Add the correct number to the empty box.

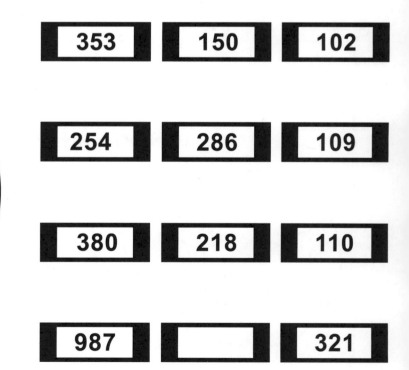

353	150	102
254	286	109
380	218	110
987		321

Can you fill in the blanks - sorry no example this time!

A

9	2	5	8	7	3
3	4	3	4	5	
2	4	3	2	2	4

B

6	3	1	7	5	2
4	2	4	3	0	8
2	4		2	4	2

C

6	3	5	6	4	9
3		4	0	2	9
2	3	2	3	3	1

D

9	7	7	5	8	9
6	8	3	5	2	1
2	2	3	3		3

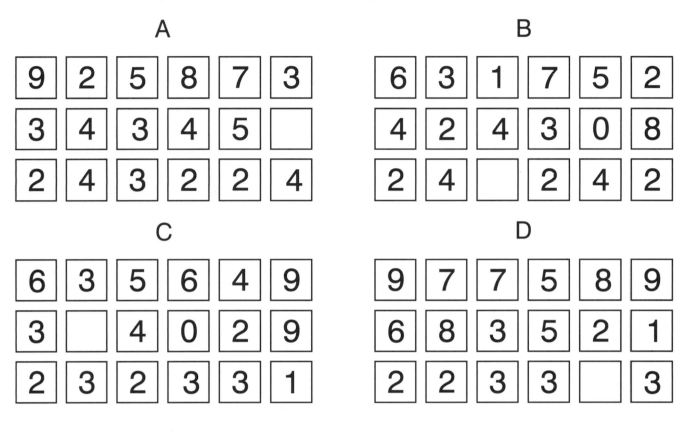

5

Which hexagon continues the sequence?

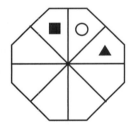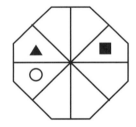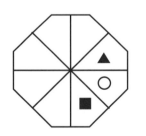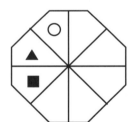

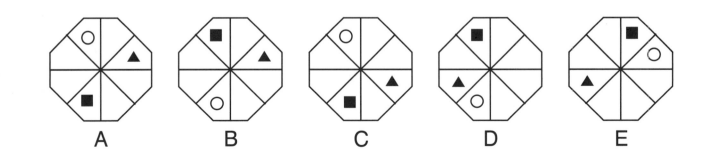

A   B   C   D   E

6

Can you replace the missing letters?

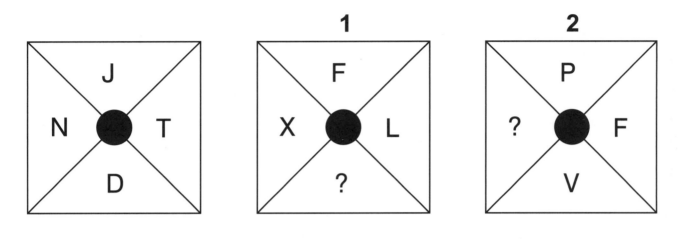

1

2

7

Can you work out what should go in the blanks?

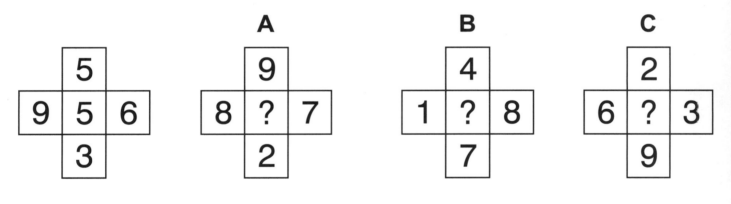

A

B

C

8

Which number replaces the blank?

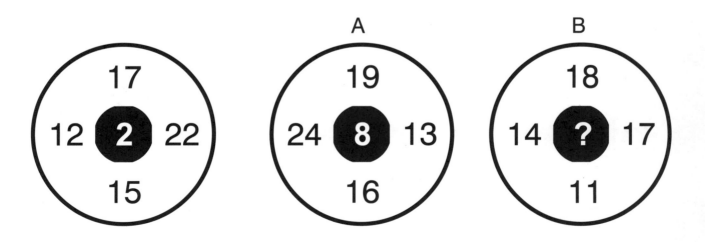

A

B

9

What time should the blank clock show?

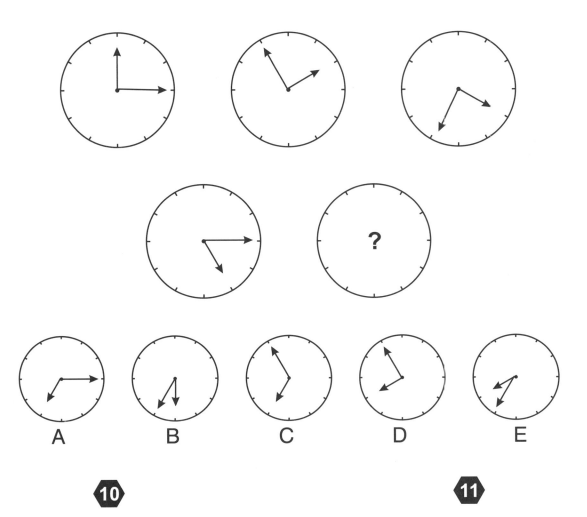

A   B   C   D   E

10

11

Whenever puzzle-loving Pam is asked her age she responds with this answer:

"I am three times older than my niece, five years ago I was five times older than her twin brother."

How old is she?

Can you complete these puzzles?

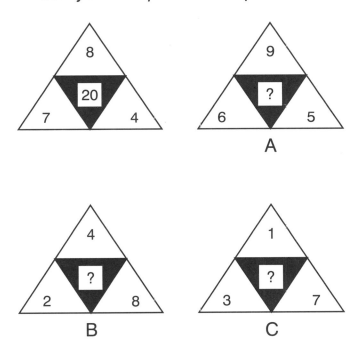

Which of the six numbered stars goes in the empty square?

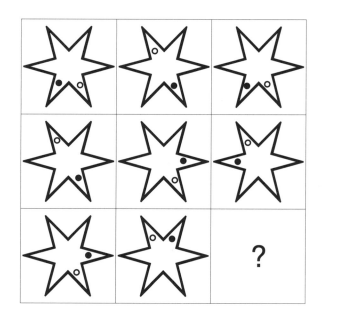

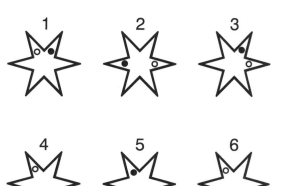

13

What letter is one up from the letter two down from the letter one down from the letter four up from the letter two up from the letter one down from the letter six down from the top letter?

A
B
C
D
E
F
G
H

14

Which number replaces the blank?

2	7	5
5	?	9
7	3	4

LEVEL 10

15

Can you insert the missing number?

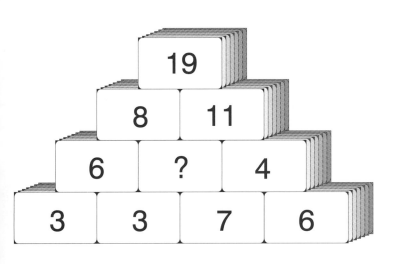

19

8 11

6 ? 4

3 3 7 6

16

Using the numbers and symbols that appear in the top line in every row and column, can you complete this puzzle?

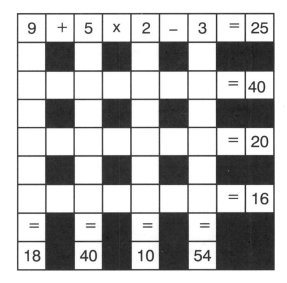

9	+	5	x	2	−	3	=	25
							=	40
							=	20
							=	16
=		=		=		=		
18		40		10		54		

17

Which number replaces the blank and completes the sequence?

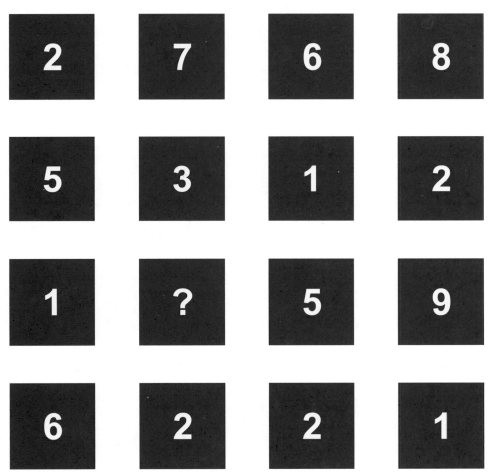

2	7	6	8
5	3	1	2
1	?	5	9
6	2	2	1

18

Which letter replaces the blank and completes the chain?

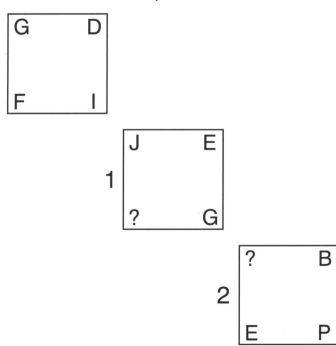

19

Can you replace the missing number?

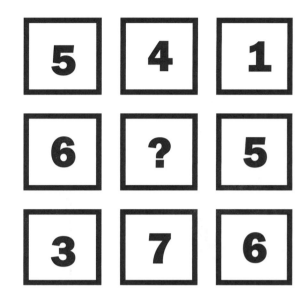

20

Which letter replaces the blanks?

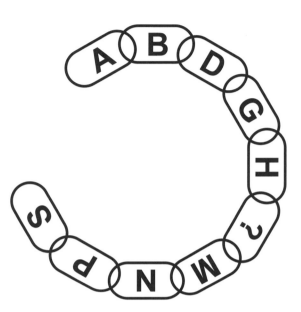

21

Can you complete the sequence?

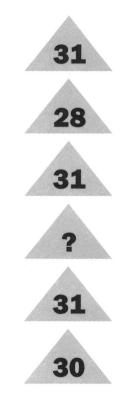

LEVEL 11

1

Which of the six numbered flowers will complete the sequence?

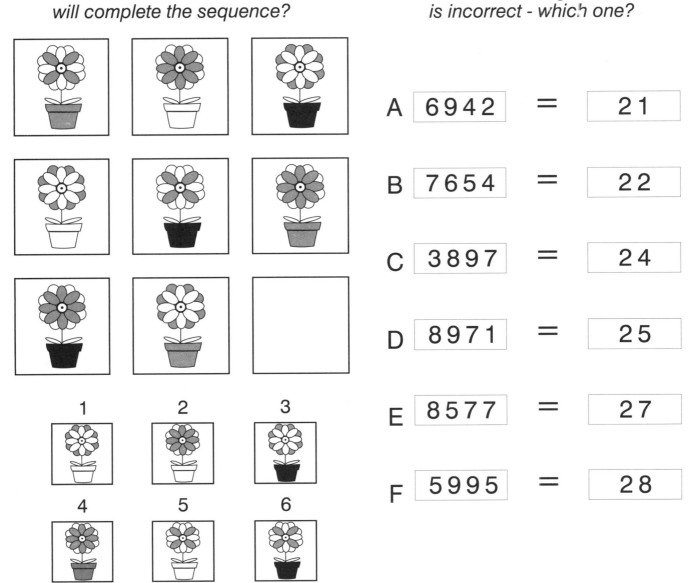

2

One of the following statements is incorrect - which one?

A 6942 = 21

B 7654 = 22

C 3897 = 24

D 8971 = 25

E 8577 = 27

F 5995 = 28

3

Can you work out which numbers are missing?

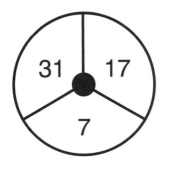

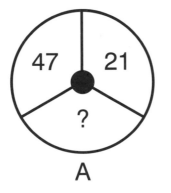

A

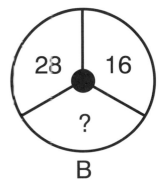

B

Which square completes the sequence?

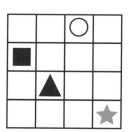
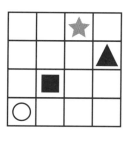
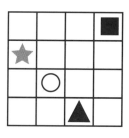
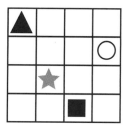

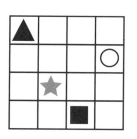
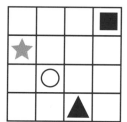
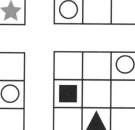
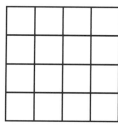

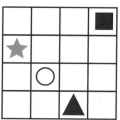
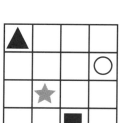
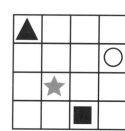
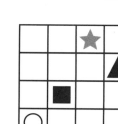

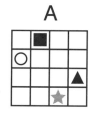
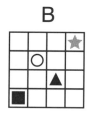
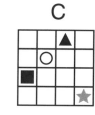

A
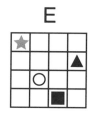

B

C

D

E

F

G

H
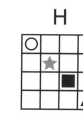

5

By following the same rule as used in each of the first three circles, can you complete the others?

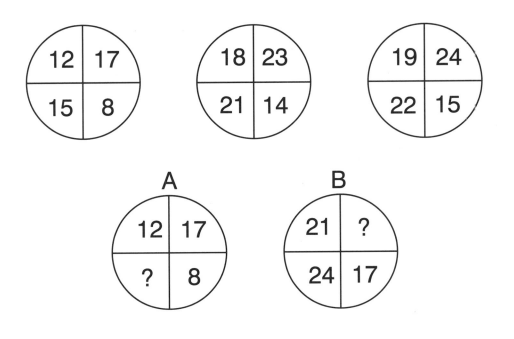

6

Which letter is missing?

7

Can you replace the question mark?

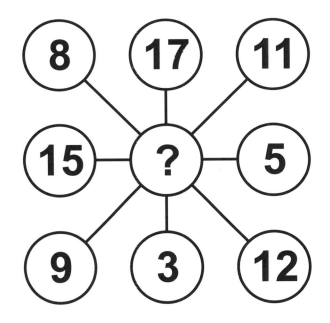

8

Draw three straight lines and separate the box into six sections, each one containing six symbols, two of each kind.

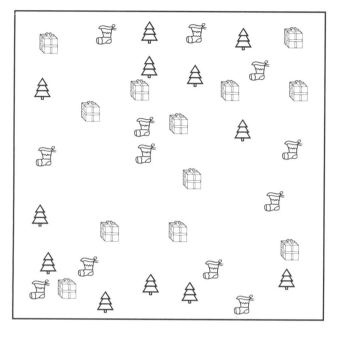

9

Each fruit represents a different number. Can you reconstruct the sum by replacing each one with a number?

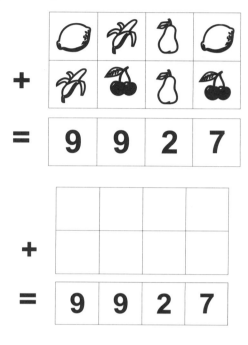

10

Can you work out which letters are missing?

 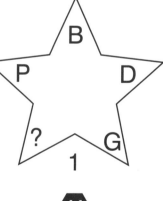 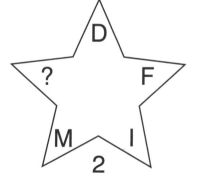

11

Can you work out which number is missing?

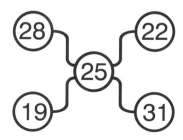 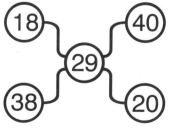 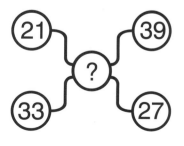

12

Can you solve this teaser?

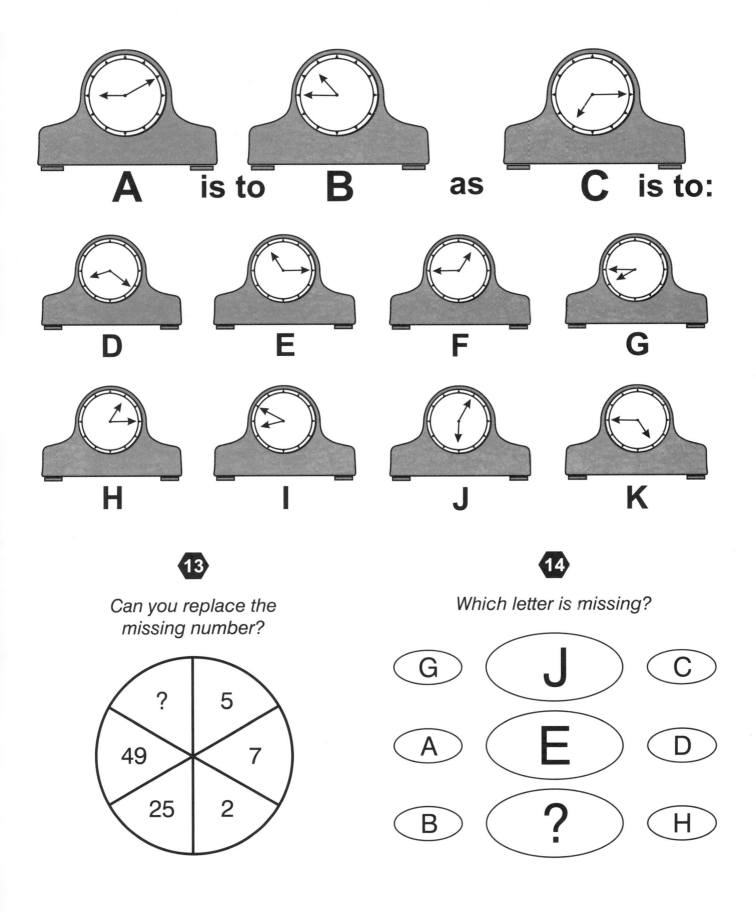

A is to **B** as **C** is to:

D   E   F   G

H   I   J   K

13

Can you replace the missing number?

?	5
49	7
25	2

14

Which letter is missing?

G   J   C

A   E   D

B   ?   H

15

Can you insert the missing numbers?

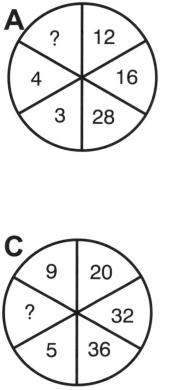

A

? | 12
4 | 16
3 | 28

B

2 | 24
1 | ?
6 | 8

C

9 | 20
? | 32
5 | 36

16

Which number is the odd one out in each group?

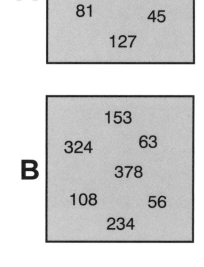

A

99
270   171
    360
81
45
127

B

153
324   63
378
108   56
234

17

Which symbol continues this sequence?

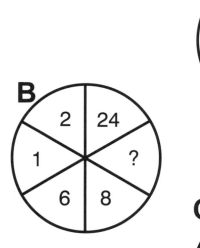   ?

1   2   3

4   5   6

Which statement is wrong?

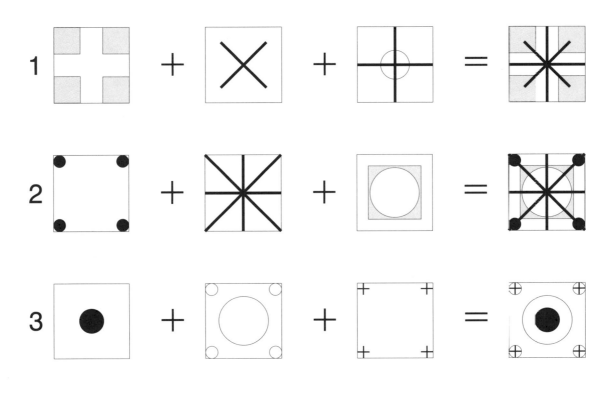

Finishing at the square with a star in it - can you find the start point in this grid?

Move one square North when you land on a square marked N1, two squares South when you land on a square marked S2 etc. etc.

3S	1W	2E	2E	1S	3W
4S	1N	★	2W	3E	5W
2E	2E	2S	1S	1E	2N
1E	1N	2N	1W	1W	1S
3E	2E	1S	1W	2N	1W
1N	1W	3E	2E	2N	2N

20

Can you fill in the blanks?

1	14	5	?	9	6
16	3	12	?	8	11

21

Which square continues the sequence?

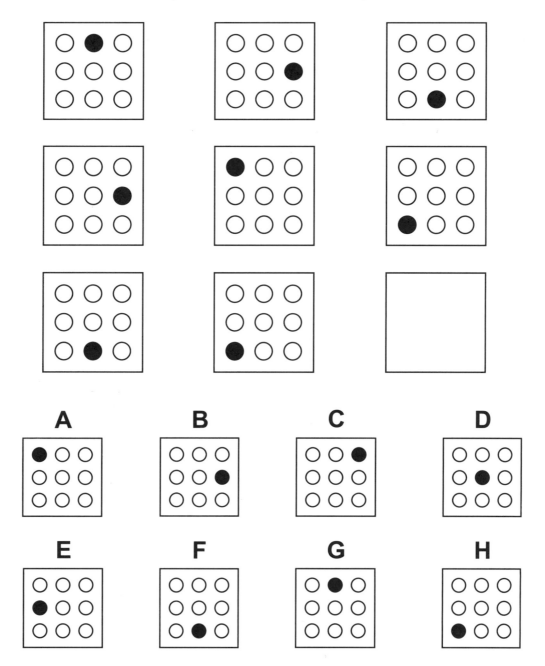

22

Which letter is missing?

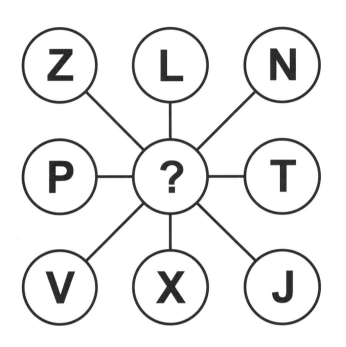

23

Can you work out the logic and solve the puzzle?

24

Can you work out which number is missing?

25

Complete the puzzle.

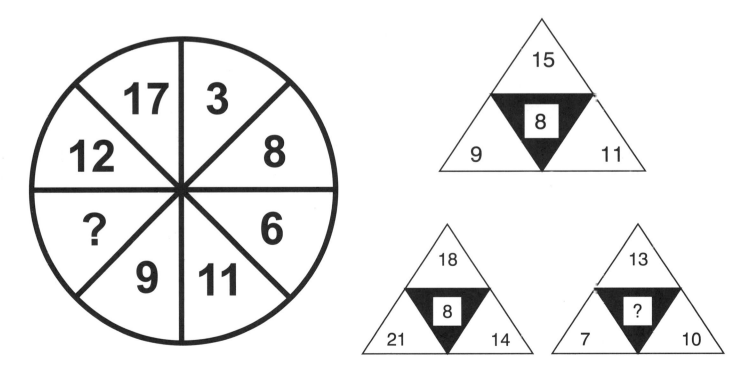

Which letter replaces the blank and completes the chain?

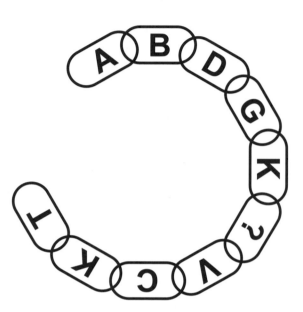

Can you replace the missing number?

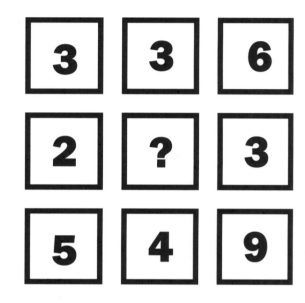

Which letter replaces the blank?

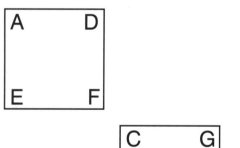

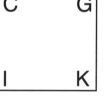

Can you complete the sequence?

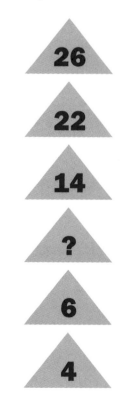

1

Which of the four numbered boxes will complete the sequence?

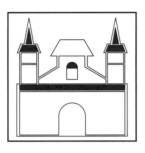 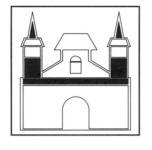 

 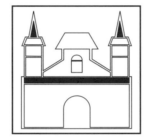 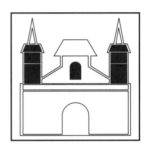

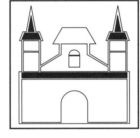  

1   2   3   4

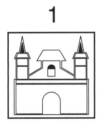 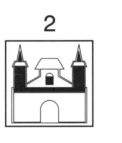 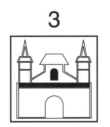 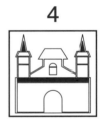

2

Can you work out which number is missing?

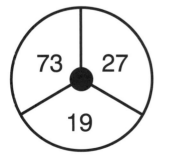 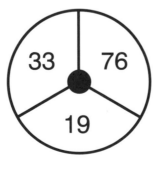 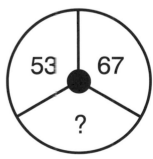

3

What time should the blank clock show?

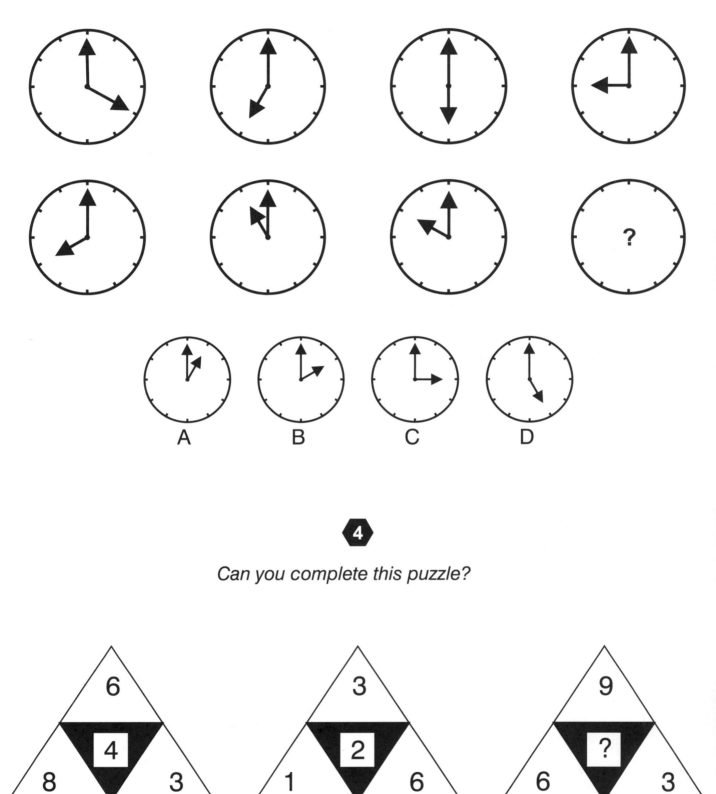

4

Can you complete this puzzle?

5

Can you fill in the missing number?

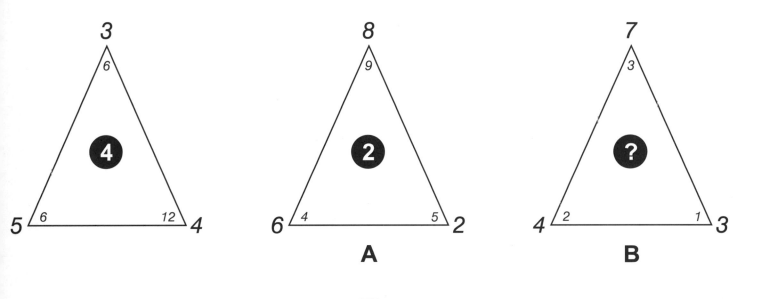

A

B

6

Can you work out which letters are missing from each line?

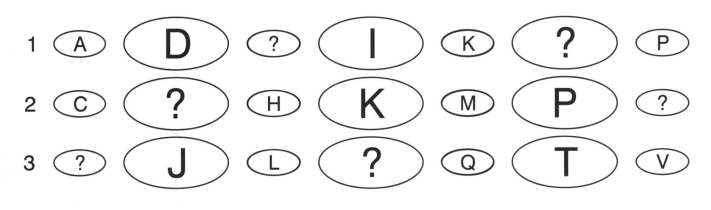

1 — A — D — ? — I — K — ? — P

2 — C — ? — H — K — M — P — ?

3 — ? — J — L — ? — Q — T — V

7

Complete this teaser

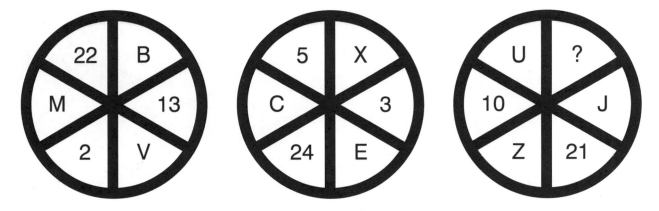

8

Which cube can be made from this shape?

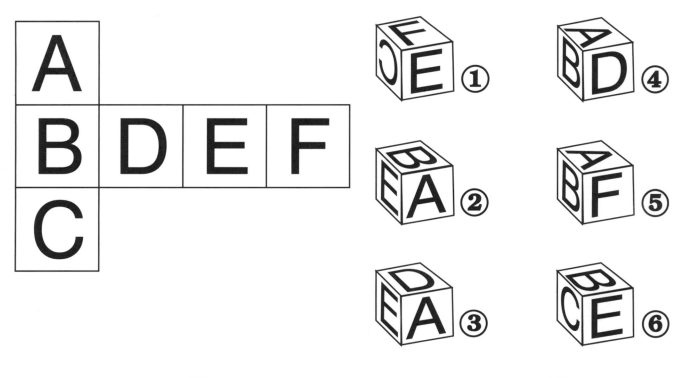

A			
B	D	E	F
C			

① ② ③ ④ ⑤ ⑥

9

Using only the letters given in the top row, complete this square so that no row, column or diagonal line contains the same letter more than once.

A	B	C	D	E
		E		
		B		
		D		
D	E	A	B	C

10

Which number is missing?

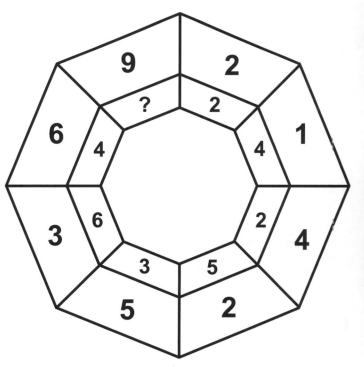

11

Can you insert the missing number?

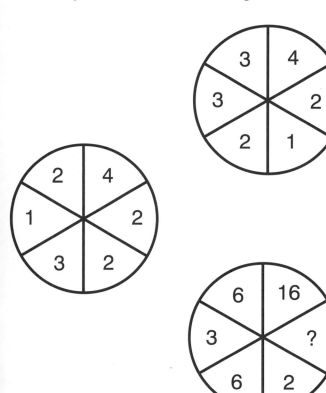

12

Which letter is the odd one out in each group?

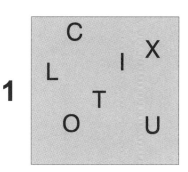

1

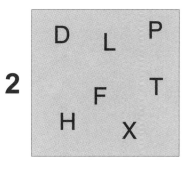

2

13

Insert the numbers 1 - 9 inclusive into the number trail to reach the answer.

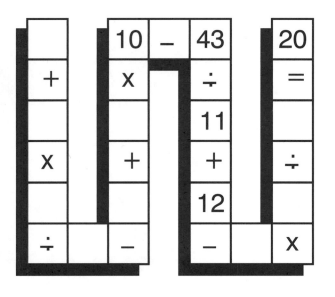

14

Which number should replace the question mark?

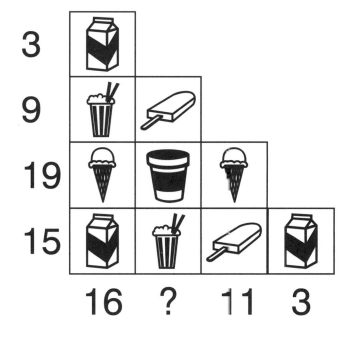

15

Study these boxes and solve the puzzle.

4	7	1
6	2	**4**

3	6	3
9	2	**5**

6	2	3
5	6	**12**

5	2	1
5	1	**8**

2	1	2
3	5	**7**

8	8	2
1	4	**?**

16

Which letter would complete this puzzle?

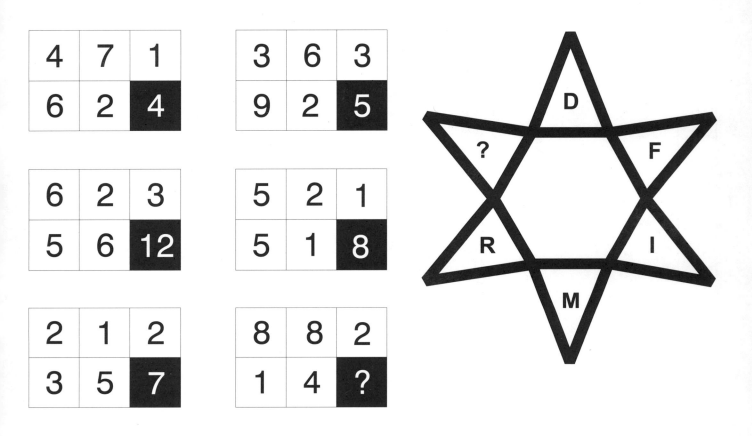

17

Can you fill in the missing number?

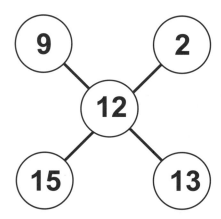

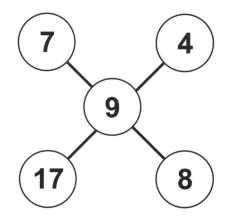

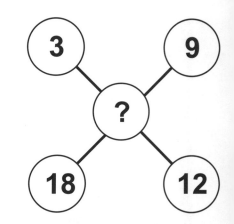

18

Which of these six watches should replace the blank one?

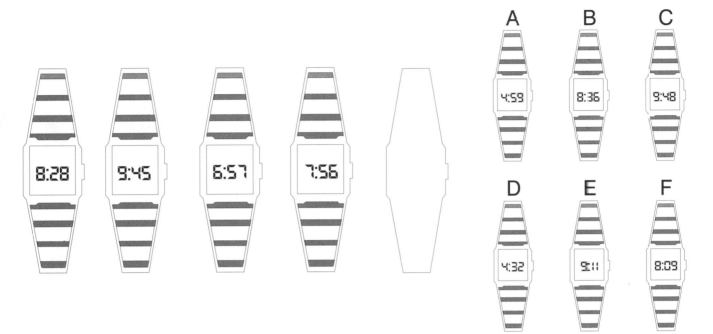

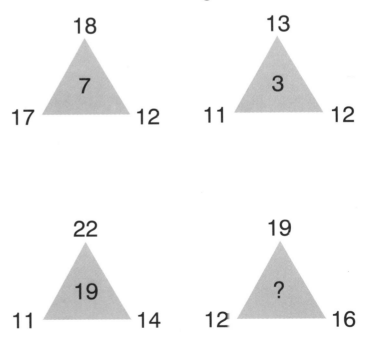

A   B   C

4:59   8:36   9:48

D   E   F

4:32   9:11   8:09

19

Can you fill in the blank?

B

?

E

G

K

M

20

Continuing the logic used in the first three puzzles, can you work out what the missing number is?

18
7
17   12

13
3
11   12

22
19
11   14

19
?
12   16

21

Can you insert the missing number?

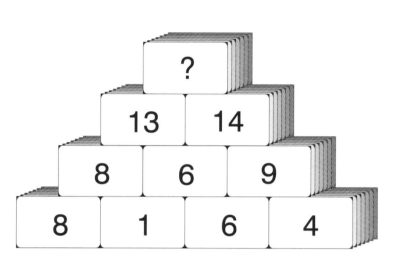

Pyramid:
- Top: ?
- 13, 14
- 8, 6, 9
- 8, 1, 6, 4

22

Using the numbers and symbols that appear in the top line in every row and column, can you complete this puzzle?

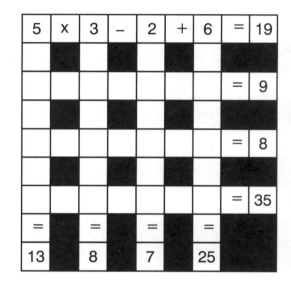

| 5 | x | 3 | – | 2 | + | 6 | = | 19 |

Down the sides:
- = 9
- = 8
- = 35

Bottom:
- = 13
- = 8
- = 7
- = 25

23

The numbers in the diagram represent a complete set of dominoes. The blank is represented by 0. Some dominoes are vertical, others are horizontal. Two dominoes have been highlighted for you but can you draw in the rest? You might find it easier using the checklist on the right.

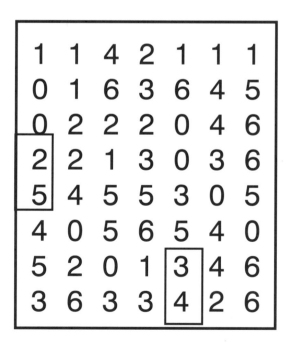

Grid:
```
1 1 4 2 1 1 1
0 1 6 3 6 4 5
0 2 2 2 0 4 6
2 2 1 3 0 3 6
5 4 5 5 3 0 5
4 0 5 6 5 4 0
5 2 0 1 3 4 6
3 6 3 3 4 2 6
```

Checklist:
0 0	2 3
0 1	2 4
0 2	2 5 ✓
0 3	2 6
0 4	3 3
0 5	3 4 ✓
0 6	3 5
1 1	3 6
1 2	4 4
1 3	4 5
1 4	4 6
1 5	5 5
1 6	5 6
2 2	6 6

24

Which letter completes the wheel?

25

Add the correct number to the empty box.

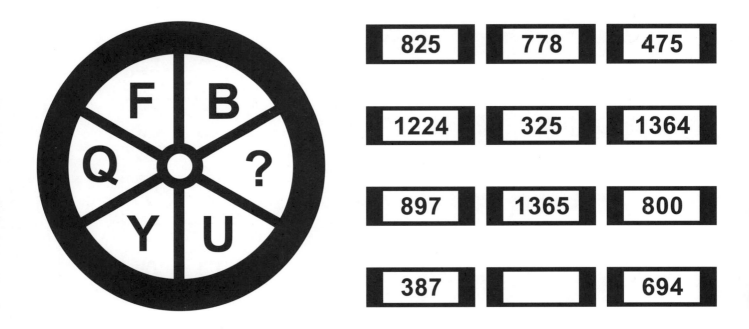

825	778	475
1224	325	1364
897	1365	800
387		694

26

Which shape continues this sequence?

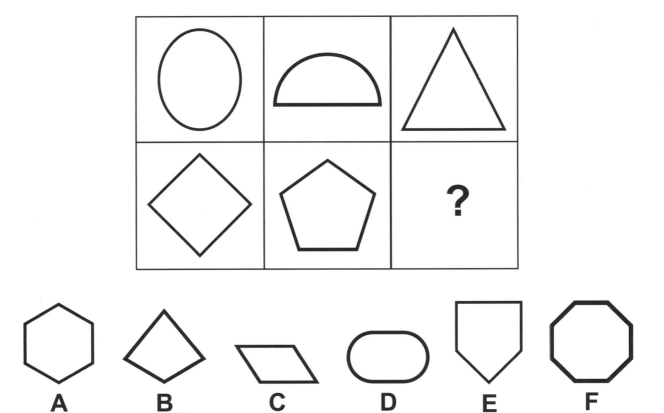

A   B   C   D   E   F

27

Which number is missing?

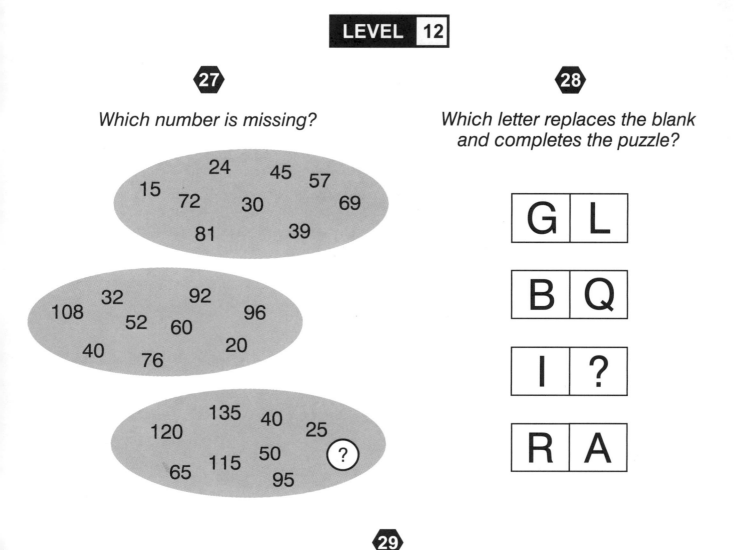

28

Which letter replaces the blank and completes the puzzle?

G	L

B	Q

I	?

R	A

29

Which square replaces the empty one?

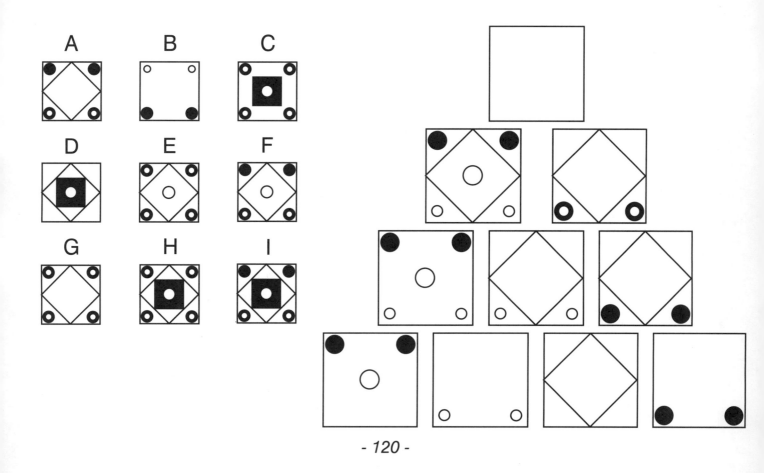

1

Which of the four numbered shapes completes the sequence?

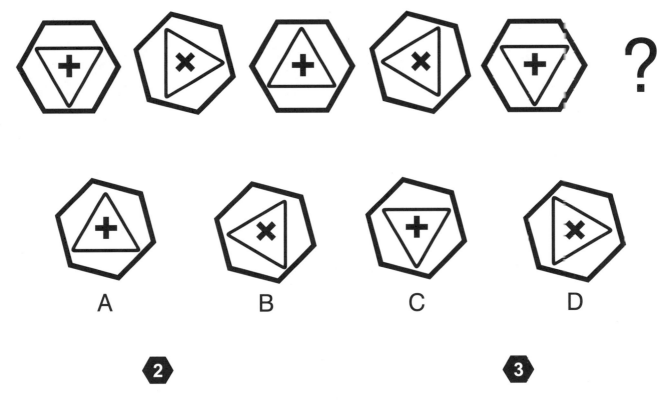

A   B   C   D

2

A mountain climber lost all of his equipment in a snow storm one day and in order to reach a place of safety he had to scale a forty foot rock face.

With no ropes or safety equipment how did he manage to do this?

3

Can you replace the missing letter?

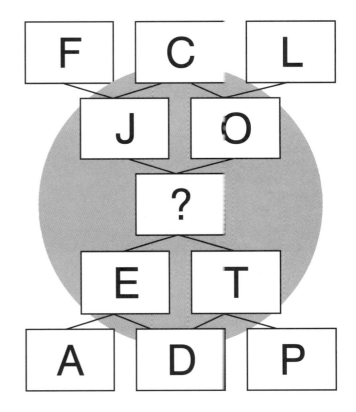

4

Which is the odd one out?

5

By using the same rule for each puzzle - can you fill in the missing numbers?

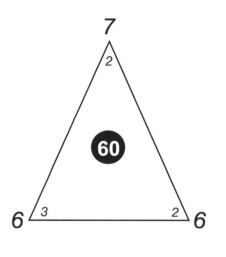

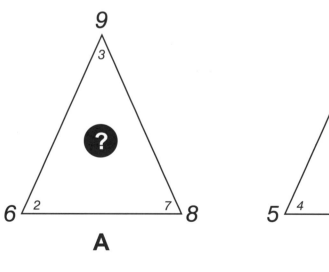

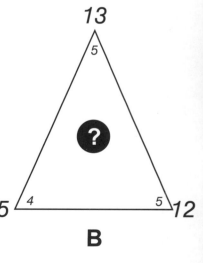

A

B

Which of the five numbered pieces goes in the shaded area?

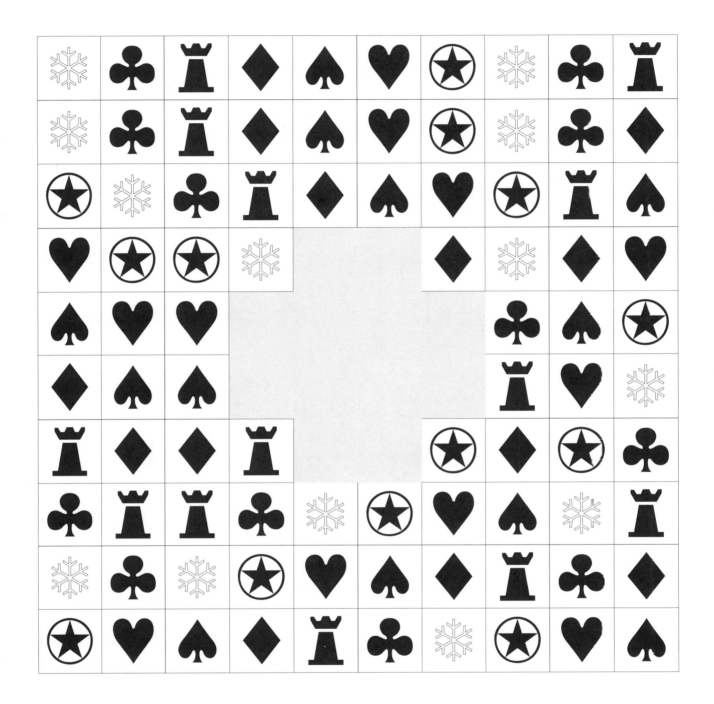

7

Can you complete these puzzles using the example given?

A		G
C	I	A
B		C

1

B		D
G	?	D
C		A

2

D		A
I	?	C
B		C

3

B		I
I	?	F
C		D

8

Fill in the missing number.

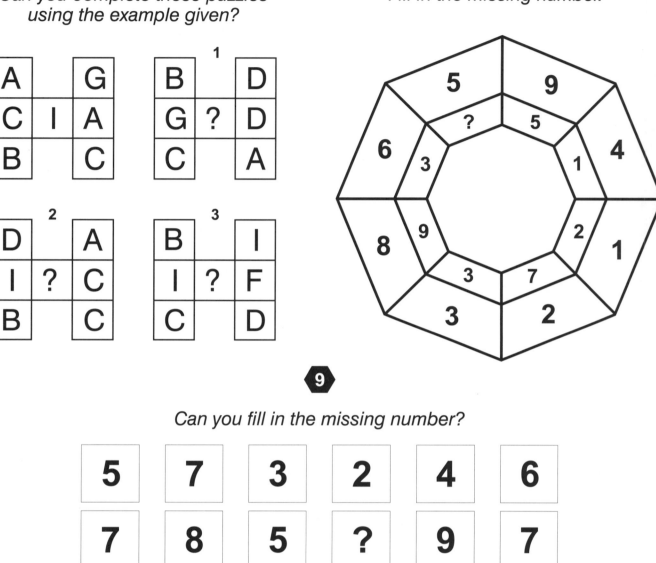

9

Can you fill in the missing number?

5	7	3	2	4	6
7	8	5	?	9	7
2	1	2	7	5	1

10

Insert the correct mathematical signs between each number.

14   3   6   47   15   39

11

Which card completes each row?

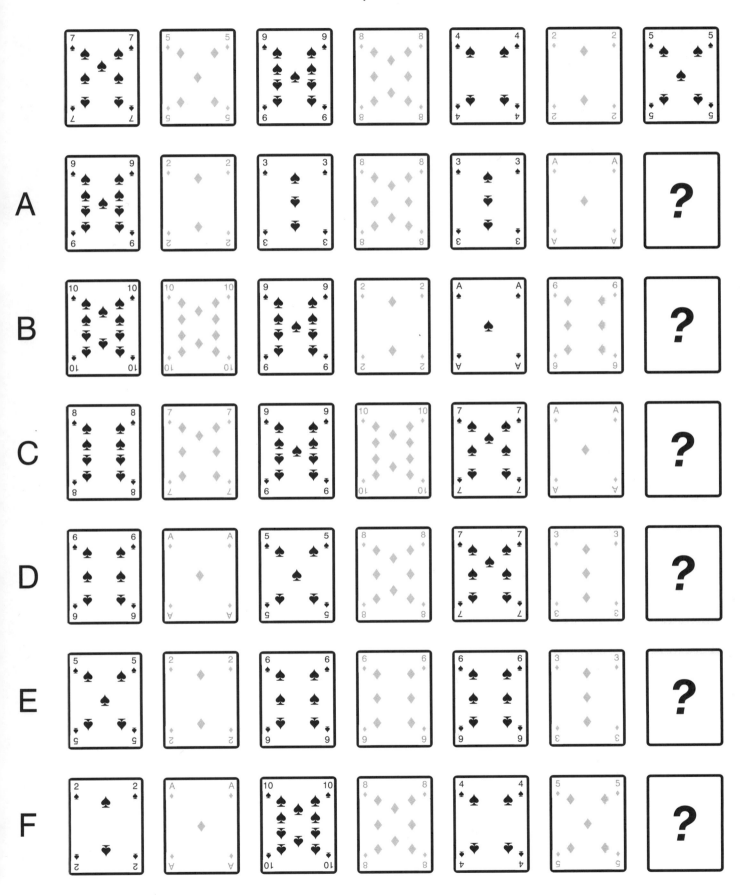

12

Which letter replaces the
question mark?

13

Can you complete this puzzle?

14

Can you fill in the blanks?

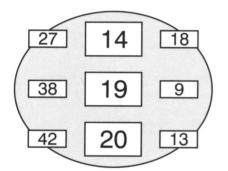

A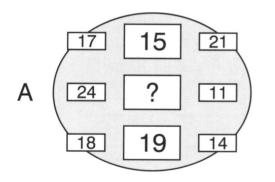

B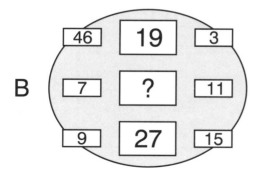

15

Study this puzzle carefully
and complete the last grid.

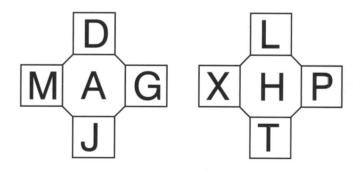

16

Can you fill in the missing numbers?

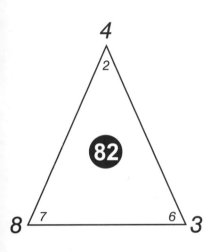

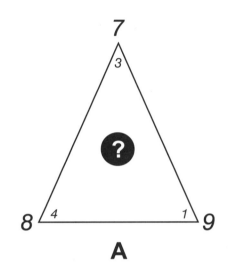

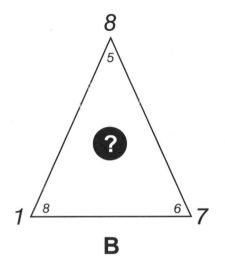

A   B

17

Complete this teaser.

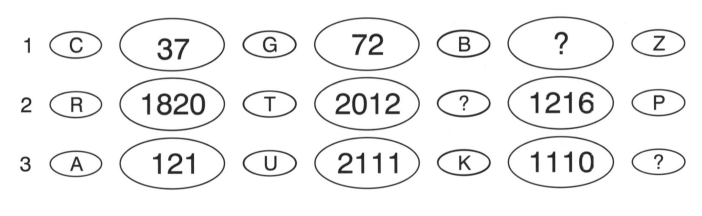

1 C 37 G 72 B ? Z

2 R 1820 T 2012 ? 1216 P

3 A 121 U 2111 K 1110 ?

18

Can you replace the missing numbers?

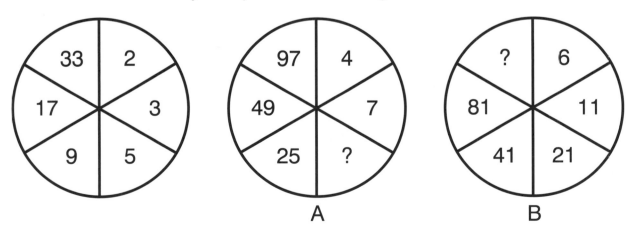

A   B

19

Can you replace the question mark?

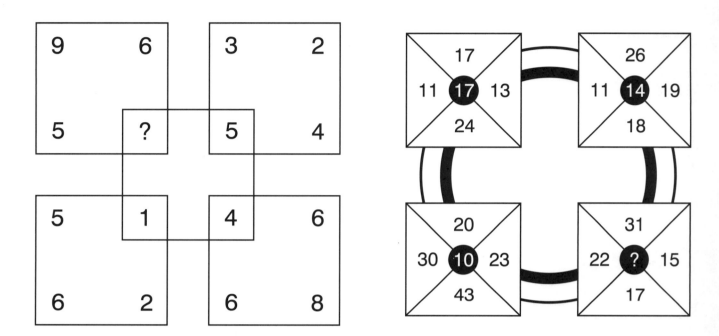

20

Can you find the missing number?

21

Which of the six numbered boxes completes the sequence?

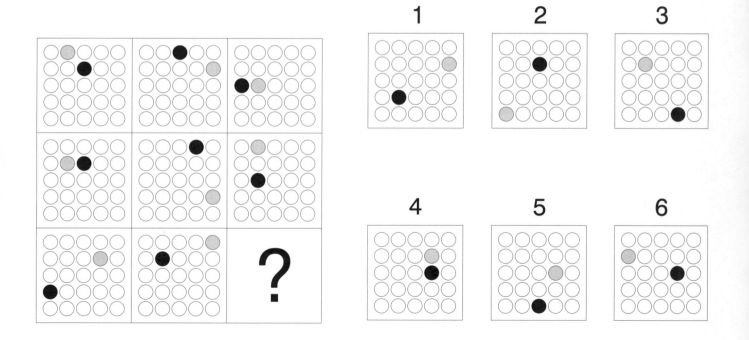

1

2

3

4

5

6

22

Insert the missing numbers.

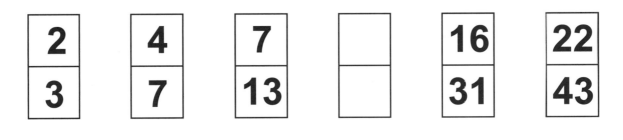

| 2 | 4 | 7 | | 16 | 22 |
| 3 | 7 | 13 | | 31 | 43 |

23

Complete the sequence of letters.

A B D D G F J H M ?

24

Which letter replaces the blank and completes the sequence?

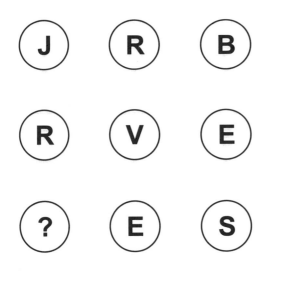

J R B

R V E

? E S

25

Can you replace the missing number?

26

Can you complete the puzzle?

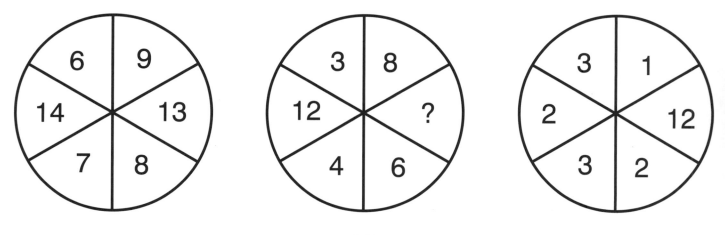

27

Can you write in the correct letters to complete the puzzle?

T	K	P	B	J	S
U	M	?	F	?	Y

28

Fill in the missing number.

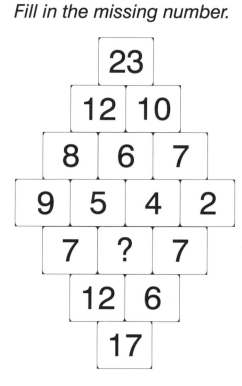

23
12 10
8 6 7
9 5 4 2
7 ? 7
12 6
17

29

Can you complete the puzzle?

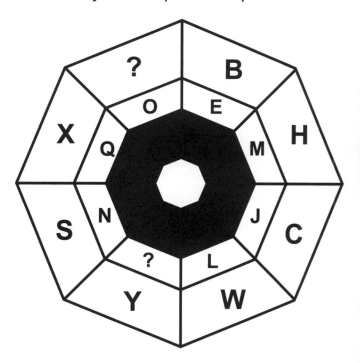

1

Which triangle is the odd one out?

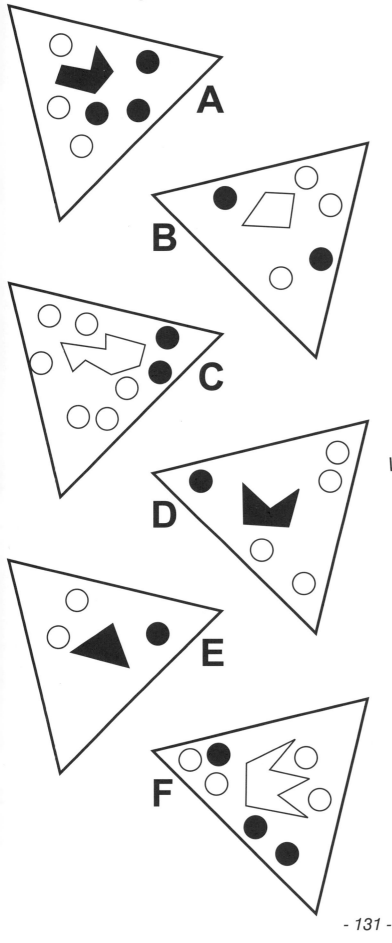

2

Can you fill in the blank?

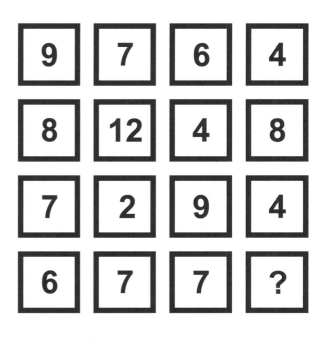

9	7	6	4
8	12	4	8
7	2	9	4
6	7	7	?

3

Which letter completes the sequence?

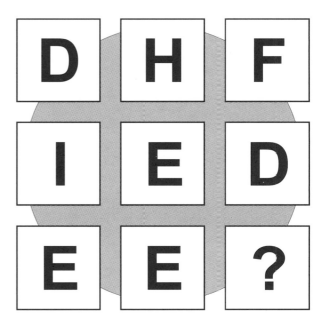

D	H	F
I	E	D
E	E	?

4

Can you fill in the blanks?

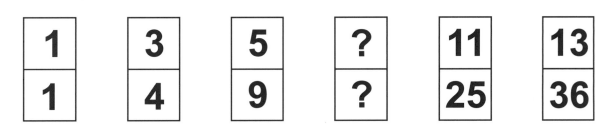

5

Which square goes in the centre?

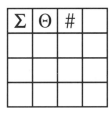
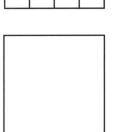
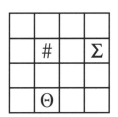
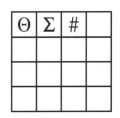

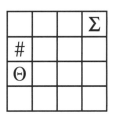
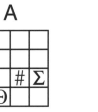
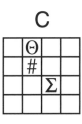

A	B	C

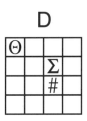
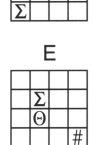

D	E	F

6

Which letter replaces the blank and completes the chain?

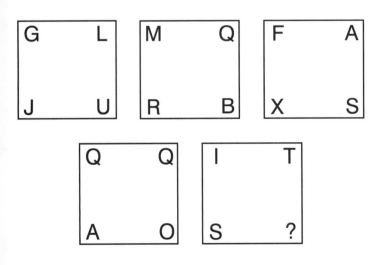

7

Can you replace the missing number?

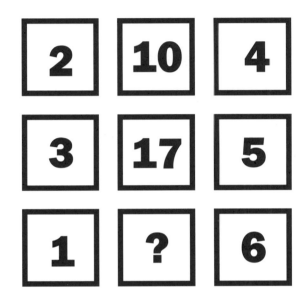

2	10	4
3	17	5
1	?	6

8

Which letter replaces the blank?

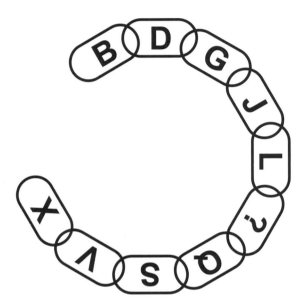

G		L
J		U

M		Q
R		B

F		A
X		S

Q		Q
A		O

I		T
S		?

9

Can you complete the sequence?

112

?

72

55

40

27

10

Which cube can be formed by folding this shape?

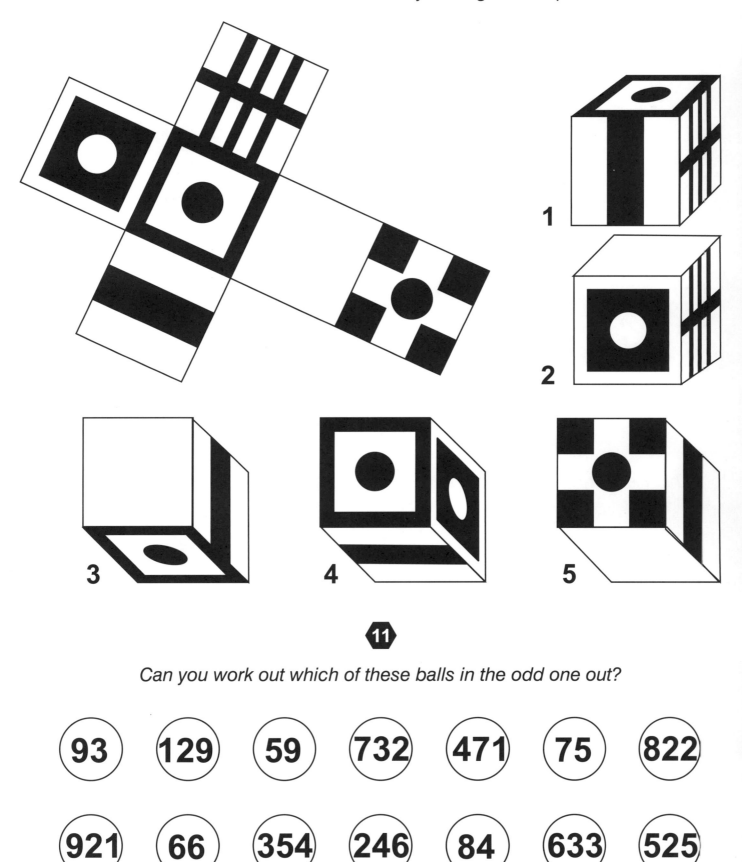

11

Can you work out which of these balls in the odd one out?

93   129   59   732   471   75   822

921   66   354   246   84   633   525

12

Using the same rule for each box can you complete this teaser?

13

Which letter is the odd one out in each circle?

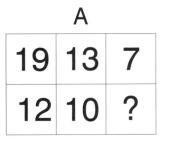

A

19	13	7
12	10	?

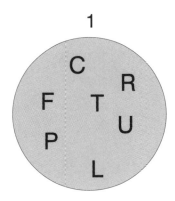

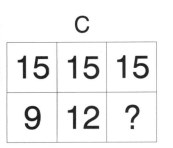

B

16	12	8
5	6	?

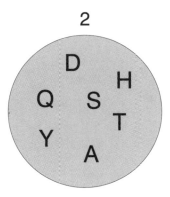

C

15	15	15
9	12	?

D

27	14	1
13	10	?

14

Can you fill in the blanks?

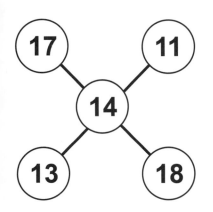

A

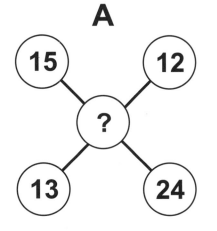

B

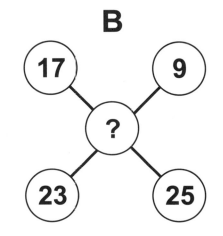

Can you fill in the missing number?

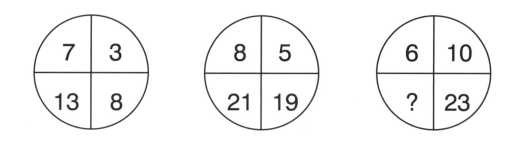

Which letter is missing?

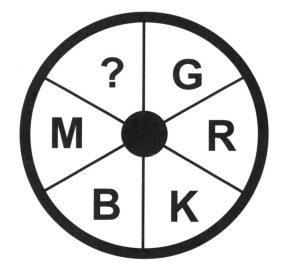

Can you replace the question mark?

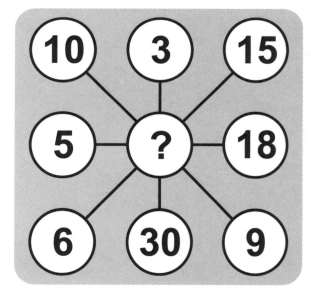

Which letter is the odd one out?

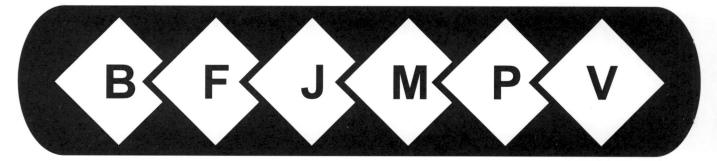

19

Which of the six numbered stars goes in the empty square?

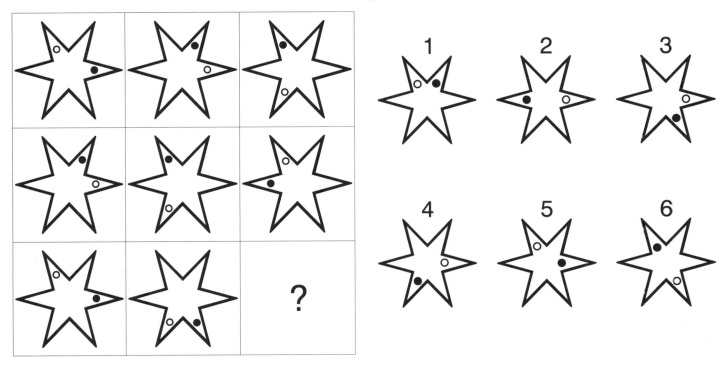

20

Which letter is two up from the letter four down from the letter one up from the letter two down from the letter five up from the letter one down from the letter which is two up from the end?

A

B

C

D

E

F

G

H

21

Which number replaces the blank?

10	16	6
20	40	?
10	24	14

22

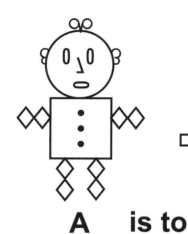
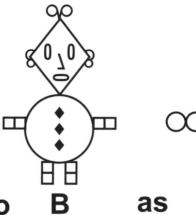
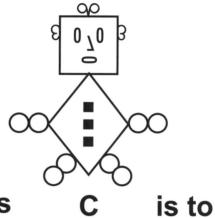

A   is to   **B**   as   **C**   is to

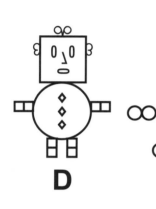
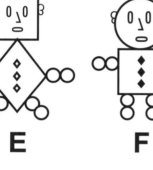

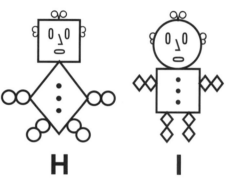

D   **E**   **F**   **G**   **H**   **I**

23

How many triangles can you count?

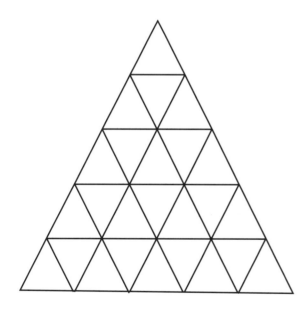

24

Every number between 0 and 9 inclusive has been used in this sum. Unfortunately some have been replaced by letters. Can you work out which number replaces each letter?

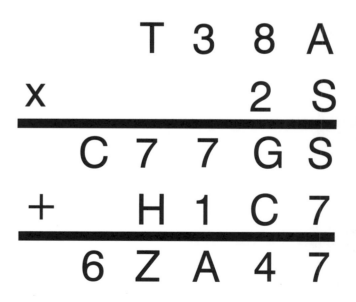

```
    T  3  8  A
 X        2  S
 ─────────────
    C  7  7  G  S
 +     H  1  C  7
 ─────────────
    6  Z  A  4  7
```

25

Replace all the numbers so that each row and column adds up to 25

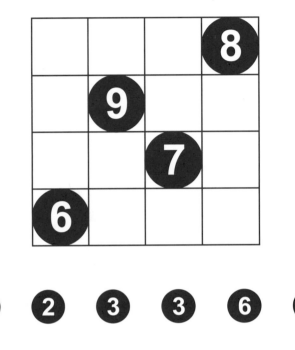

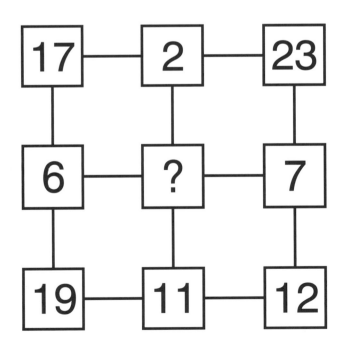

2 2 3 3 6 6

7 8 8 9 10 12

27

Which letter is missing?

17	2	23
6	?	7
19	11	12

26

What does J equal?

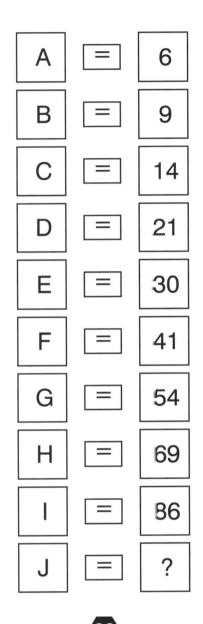

A	=	6
B	=	9
C	=	14
D	=	21
E	=	30
F	=	41
G	=	54
H	=	69
I	=	86
J	=	?

28

Which number is the odd one out?

24 46 38 17

15 78 61 36

29

Which number completes this puzzle?

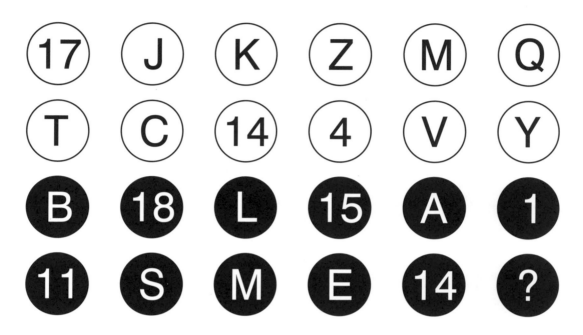

17	J	K	Z	M	Q
T	C	14	4	V	Y
B	18	L	15	A	1
11	S	M	E	14	?

30

Which letter replaces the blank and completes the sequence?

B E I N ? A I R B M

31

Which numbers replace the blanks?

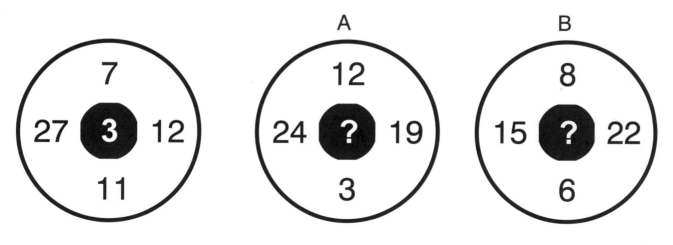

	A	B
7	12	8
27 3 12	24 ? 19	15 ? 22
11	3	6

1

Which of the six numbered shapes goes in the empty square?

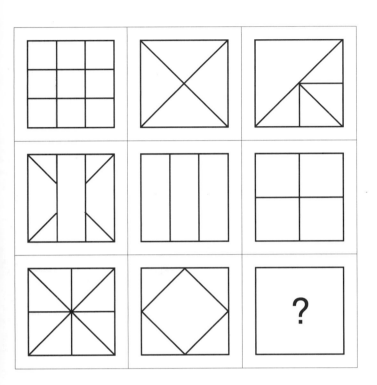

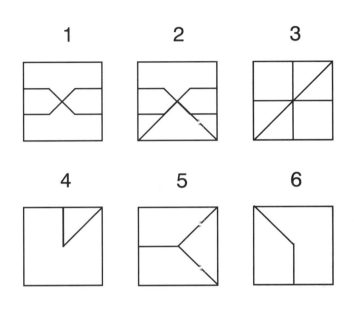

2

Which number finishes this sequence?

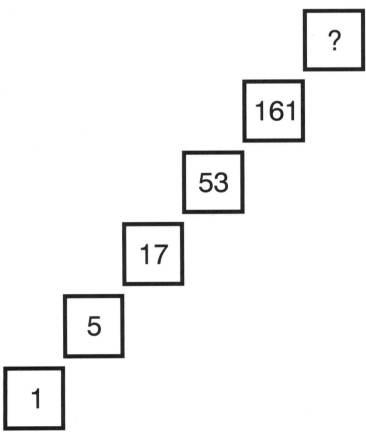

3

Can you fill in the blanks?

4

Can you insert the missing number?

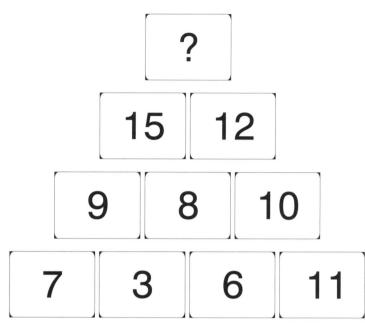

?

15	12

9	8	10

7	3	6	11

5

Using the numbers and symbols that appear in the top line in every row and column, can you complete this puzzle?

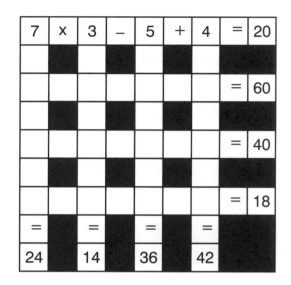

7	x	3	–	5	+	4	=	20
	■		■		■		■	
							=	60
	■		■		■		■	
							=	40
	■		■		■		■	
							=	18
=	■	=	■	=		=		
24	■	14	■	36	■	42	■	

6

This pile of dominoes is not the disorganised mess it looks. It is actually a complete set but can you work out the formation. Some blocks are horizontal, others are vertical. You will find it easier to use the checklist on the right.

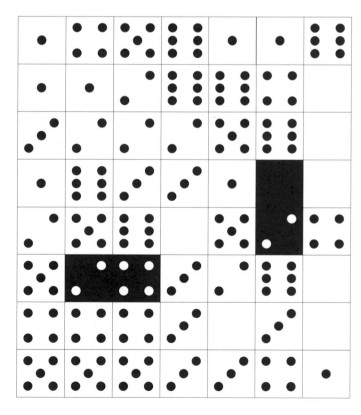

0	0			2	3	
0	1			2	4	✓
0	2	✓		2	5	
0	3			2	6	
0	4			3	3	
0	5			3	4	
0	6			3	5	
1	1			3	6	
1	2			4	4	
1	3			4	5	
1	4			4	6	
1	5			5	5	
1	6			5	6	
2	2			6	6	

7

Which of these six watches should replace the blank one?

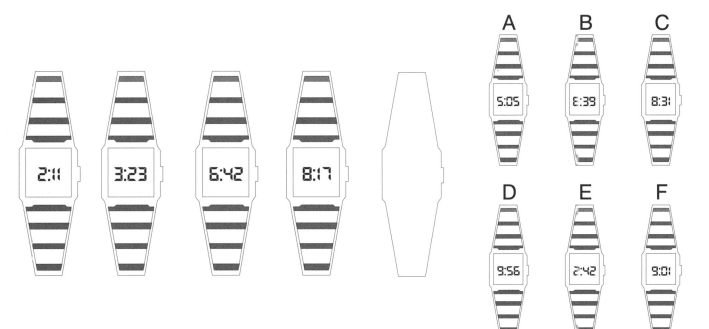

A	B	C
5:05	8:39	8:38
D	E	F
9:56	2:42	9:01

Watches: 2:11 | 3:23 | 6:42 | 8:17 | (blank)

8

Can you fill in the blanks?

A	F	?	P	Z
F	R	C	B	T
G	?	U	K	Y
P	B	?	I	D
?	T	Y	D	E

9

Can you work out which number is missing?

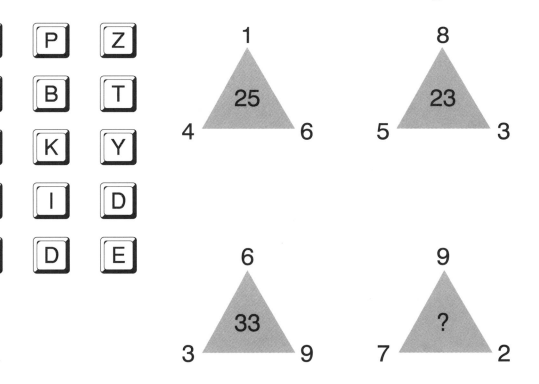

1 — 25 — 4, 6

8 — 23 — 5, 3

6 — 33 — 3, 9

9 — ? — 7, 2

10

Can you replace the missing letters?

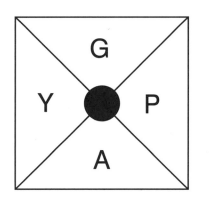
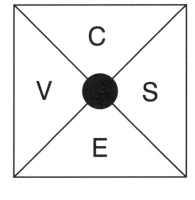
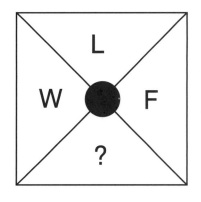

11

Can you work out the logic and solve this puzzle?

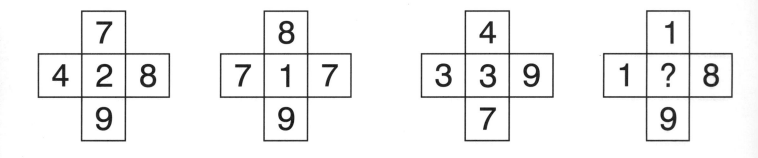

12

Which number replaces the blank?

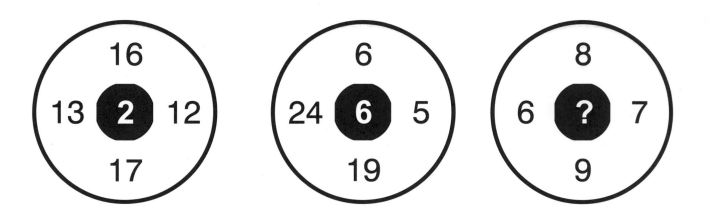

13

Which letter replaces the blank and completes the sequence?

14

Can you complete this number square?

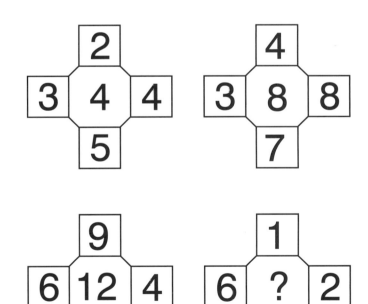

15

Can you fill in the blanks?

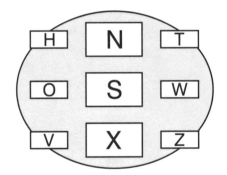

A

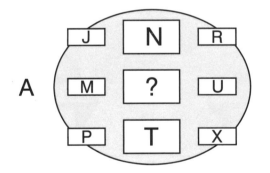

B

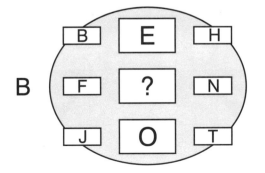

16

Study the example puzzles and, by using the same rule, can you complete the last puzzle?

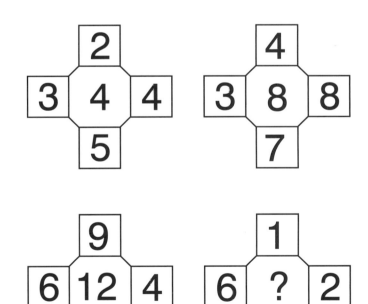

17

What time should the blank clock show?

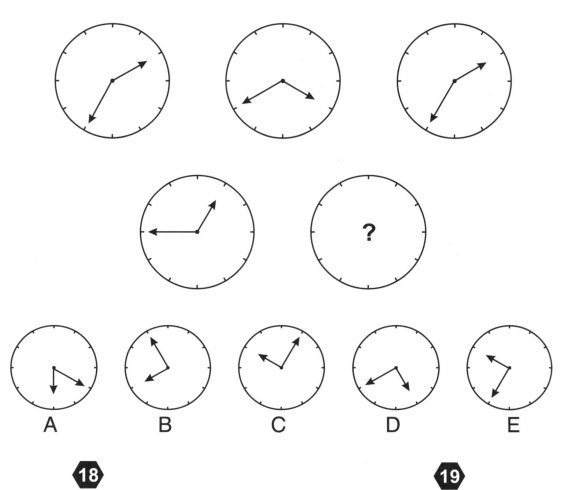

A   B   C   D   E

18

Can you complete these puzzles using the example given?

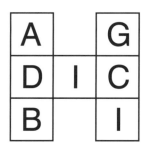

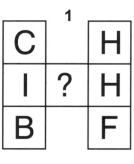

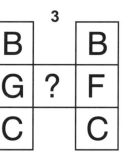

19

Can you complete these puzzles?

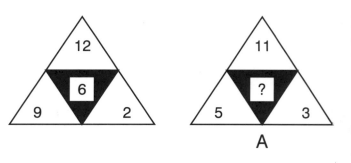

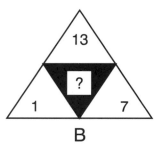

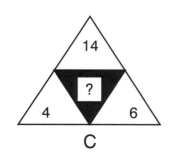

20

By following the same rule as used in each of the first four circles, can you complete the fifth circle?

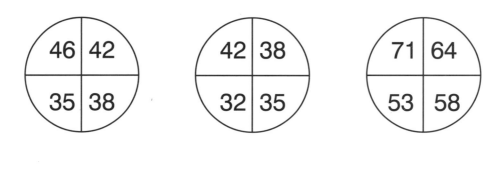

46	42
35	38

42	38
32	35

71	64
53	58

95	86
71	78

27	25
21	?

21

Which letter is missing?

22

Which number should logically go in the centre?

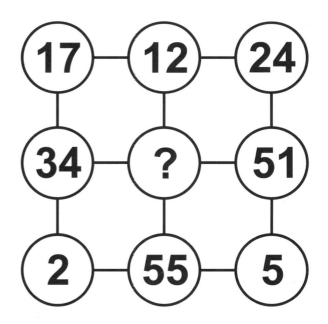

23

Which creature continues the sequence?

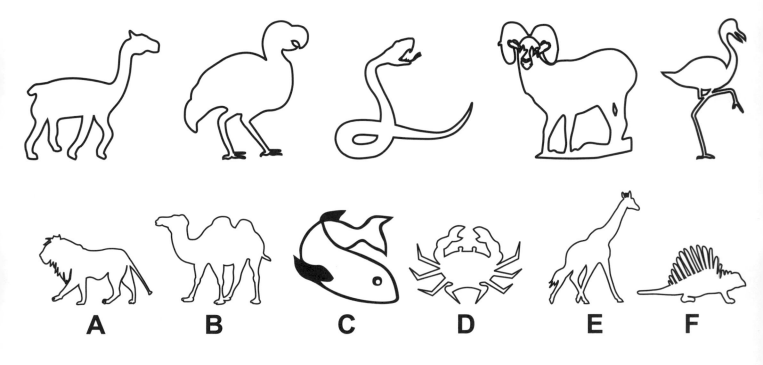

A   **B**   **C**   **D**   **E**   **F**

24

Which letter replaces the blank and completes the sequence?

Q F G C N
D W M B X
K L H E R
Z J V T Y
S A P O I
?

25

Can you replace the missing number?

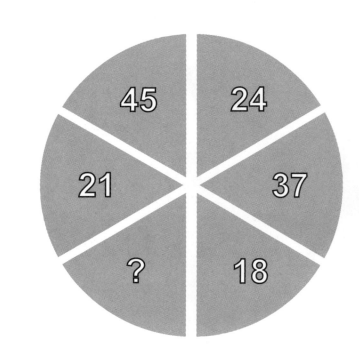

45   24
21   37
?   18

26

Can you replace the question mark?

```
6      4        9        13
9    5    ?    7
4  1  7  3
3    8    12    6
```

27

Can you find the missing numbers?

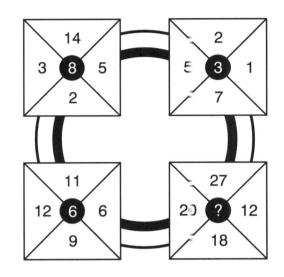

28

Which letter completes this puzzle?

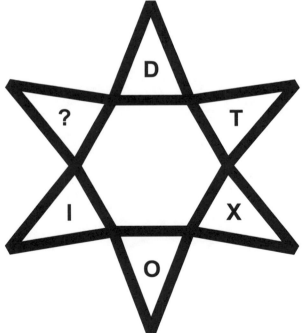

29

Which letter is missing?

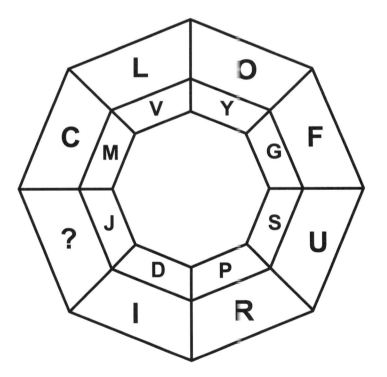

30

Follow the paths to connect each baby with the correct mode of transport.

LEVEL 16

1

Which square replaces the empty one?

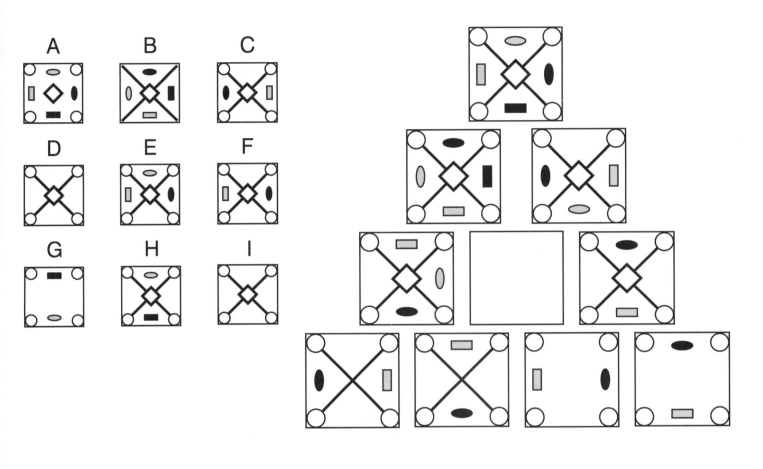

A   B   C

D   E   F

G   H   I

2

In ten years time the combined age of Mary and Jane and their brothers Paul and Phillip will be 100.

What will it be in seven years time?

3

Fill in the missing number to complete the puzzle.

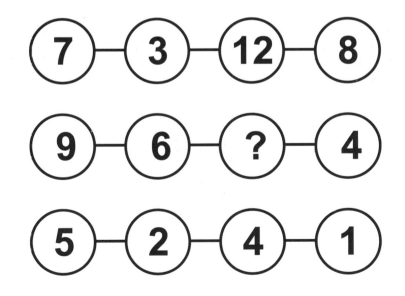

Using these six matches can you make three squares of equal size?

By adding every number between 1 - 20, can you complete this number square so that each horizontal, diagonal and corner-to-corner line equals 65?

25	22			
				23
21			24	

Which box continues this sequence?

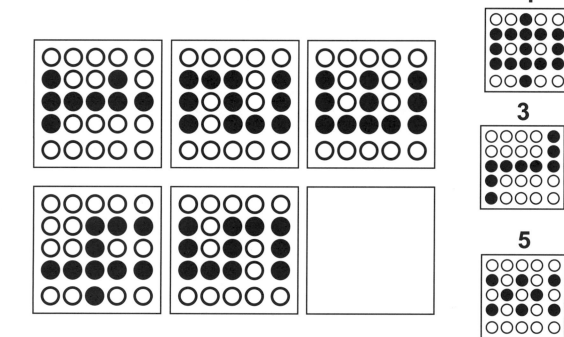

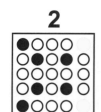

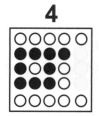

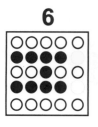

7

Can you insert the missing number?

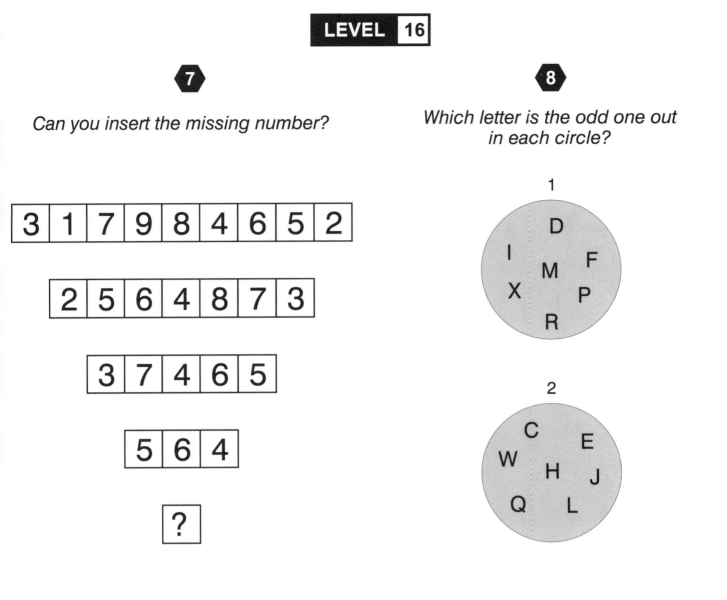

| 3 | 1 | 7 | 9 | 8 | 4 | 6 | 5 | 2 |

| 2 | 5 | 6 | 4 | 8 | 7 | 3 |

| 3 | 7 | 4 | 6 | 5 |

| 5 | 6 | 4 |

| ? |

8

Which letter is the odd one out in each circle?

1

D
I   F
M
X   P
R

2

C
W   E
H   J
Q   L

9

What number completes the puzzle?

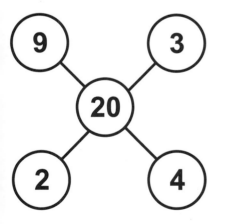

9   3
20
2   4

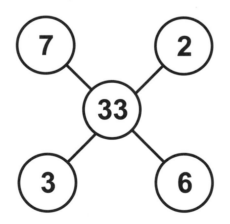

7   2
33
3   6

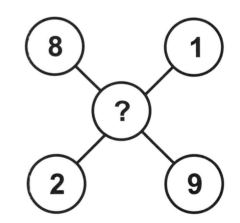

8   1
?
2   9

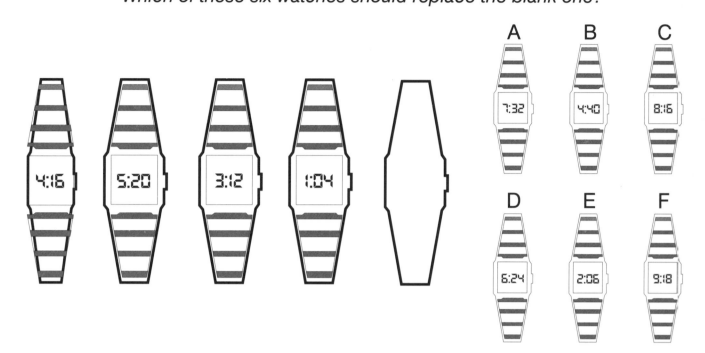

10

Which of these six watches should replace the blank one?

A 7:32 B 4:40 C 8:16 D 6:24 E 2:06 F 9:18

(watches: 4:16, 5:20, 3:12, 1:04, blank)

11

Can you fill in the blank?

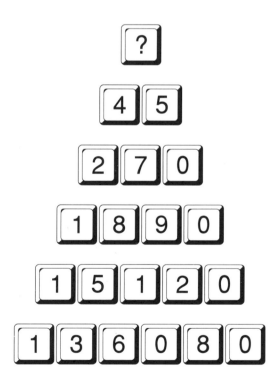

?

4 5

2 7 0

1 8 9 0

1 5 1 2 0

1 3 6 0 8 0

12

What number should replace the question mark?

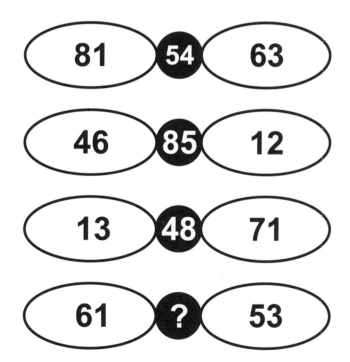

81 54 63

46 85 12

13 48 71

61 ? 53

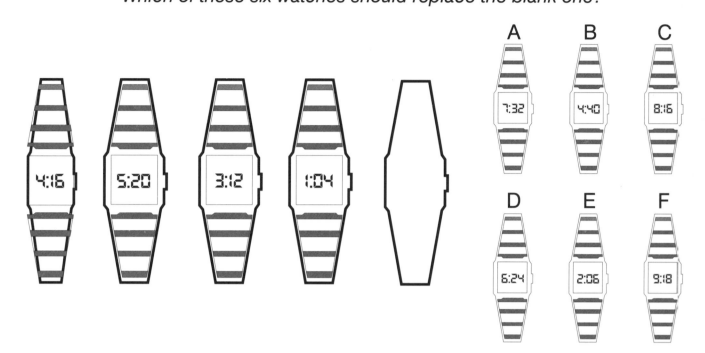

- 154 -

13

Which number completes the puzzle?

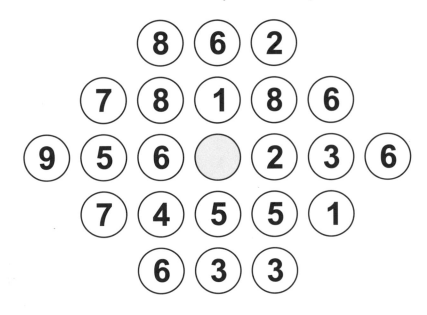

14

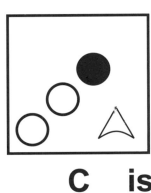

A   is to   **B**   as   **C**   is to

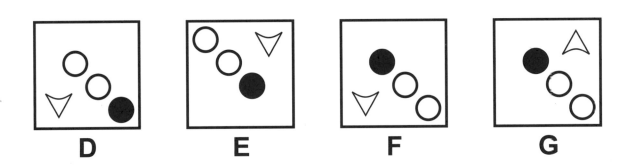

D   **E**   **F**   **G**

LEVEL 16

15

Complete this logical puzzle.

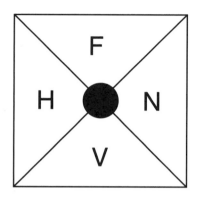

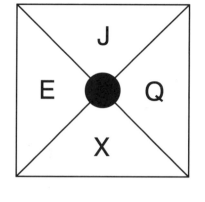

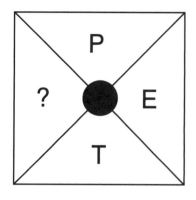

16

Can you work out what number completes the puzzle?

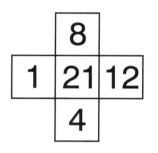

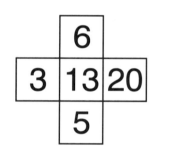

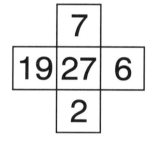

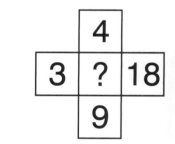

17

Which alien is the odd one out?

A

B

C

D

E

F

G

H

18

Which number is missing?

2	6
12	5

9	14
20	7

16	11
30	18

28	17
?	30

19

Which letter is missing?

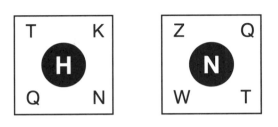

20

Which playing card continues this sequence?

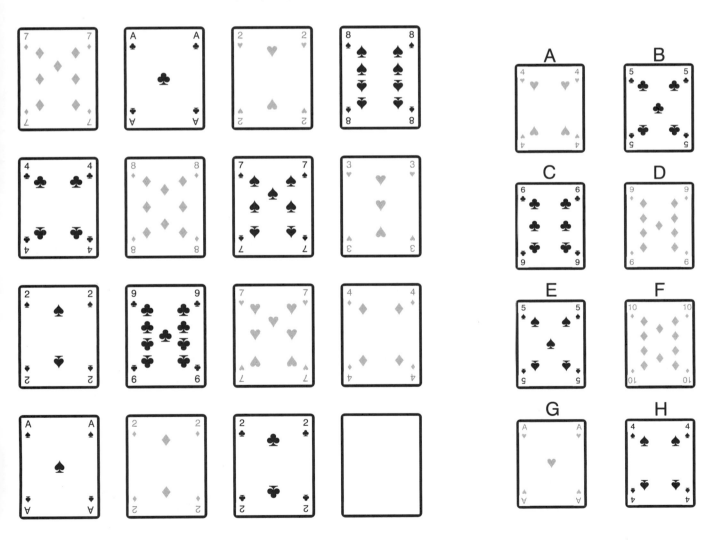

21

Which letter completes the sequence?

22

Add the correct number to the empty box.

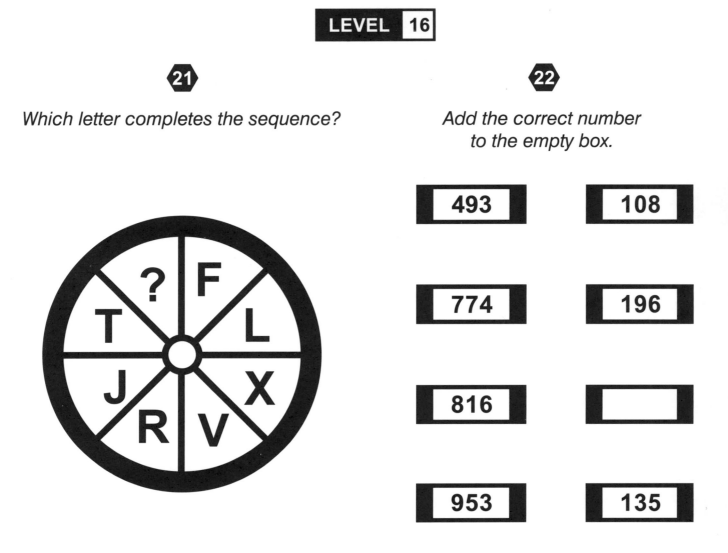

493	108
774	196
816	
953	135

23

Which shape goes in the empty box?

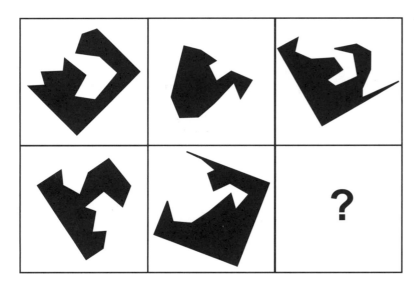

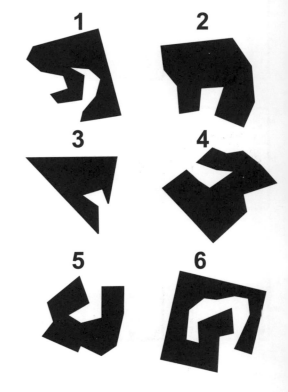

24

Draw an equilateral triangle that leaves the same number of triangles inside as it does outside. It must not overlap any other triangle or the outside of the box.

25

Which number comes next in this sequence?

?
93
57
32
16
7
3

26

Insert the missing number.

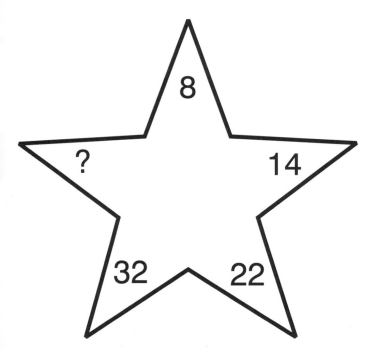

27

Every number between 1 and 16 should be put into this grid so that each row, column and diagonal adds up to 34. Some letters have already been added to give you a start.

			16
	12		
4			
		8	

28

Can you replace the question mark?

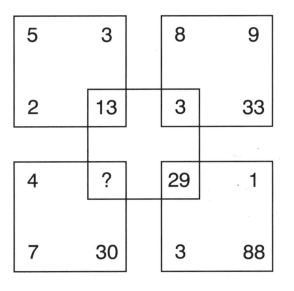

29

Can you find the missing number?

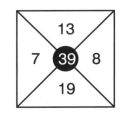
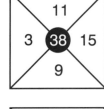
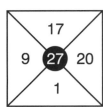
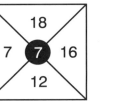
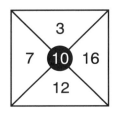
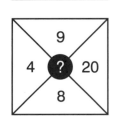

30

Which letter is missing?

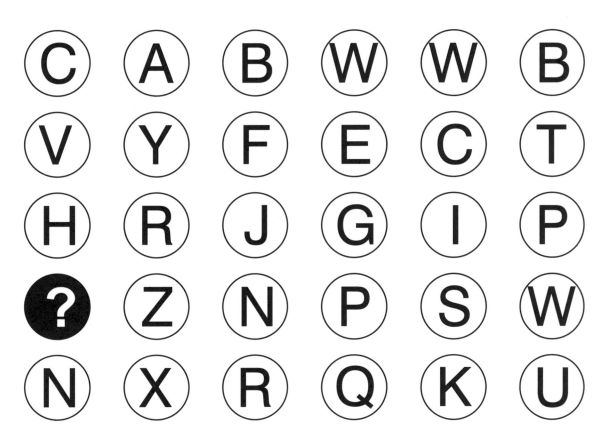

1

Which of the six numbered shapes is the odd man out?

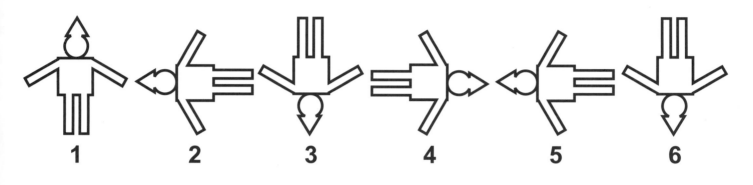

2

Insert the missing number.

3

Which of these six sections will complete the puzzle?

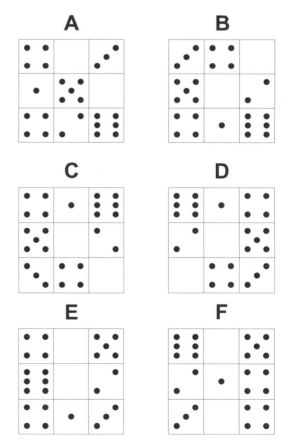

4

Can you insert the missing number?

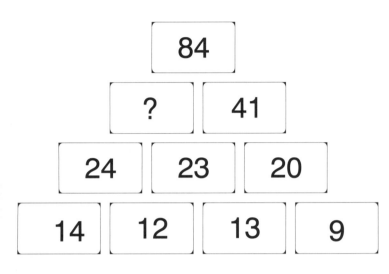

5

Move four matches and make three equilateral triangles.

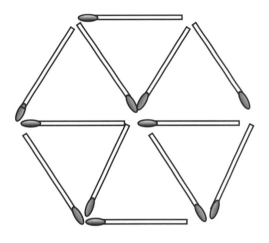

6

All of these pieces, except one, will form a square when correctly replaced back into the grid. Can you work out which is the extra piece?

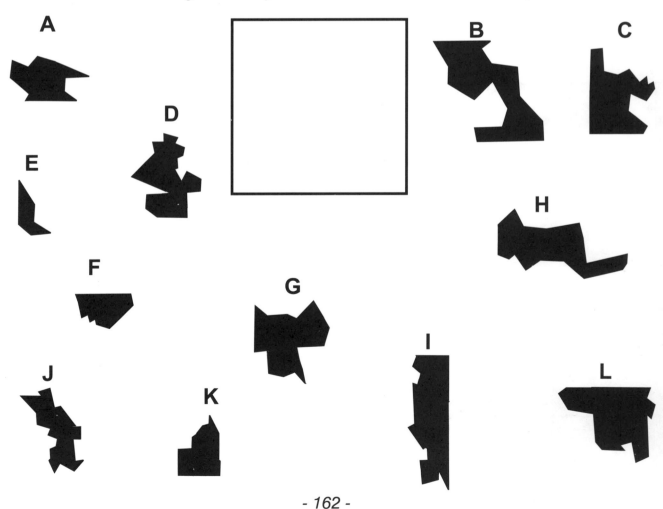

7

Which of these shapes is the odd one out?

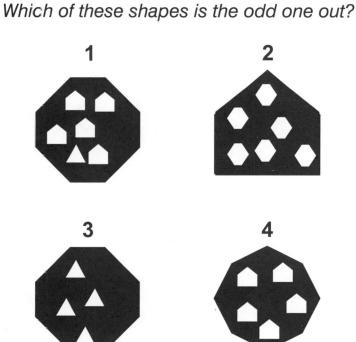

1 2

3 4

5 6

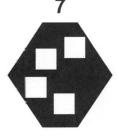

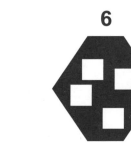

7 8

9 10

8

Complete this puzzle.

87   19

89   25   17

16   99   7

?

9

Mrs Smith, the head teacher of the local primary school was about to retire. On her last day, she bought 10 boxes of toffees, each containing between 50 and 60 sweets.

Each child received more than one sweet but less than forty.

From the information given, can you work out how many pupils were at the school and how many sweets each one received?

10

Use eleven of these letters and return
the puzzle back to its original form.

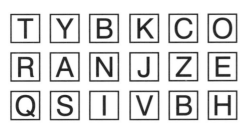

11

Which number is missing?

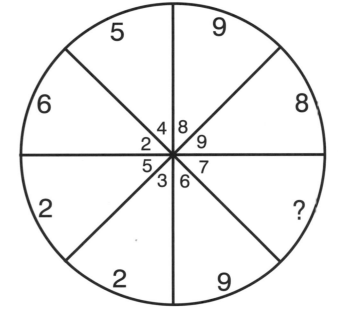

12

Which letter completes this puzzle?

13

Which letter is missing?

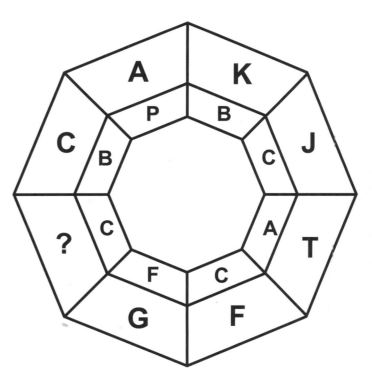

14

Which of these six watches should replace the blank one?

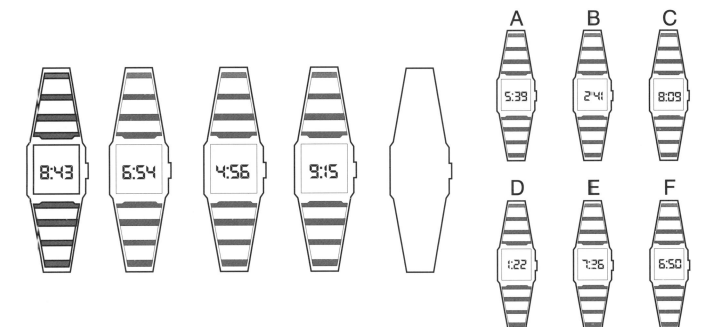

15

Can you fill in the blank?

16

Can you work out which number is missing?

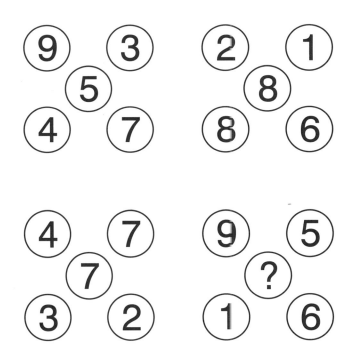

17

Which square is the odd one out?

1 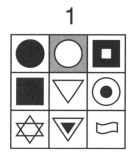 2 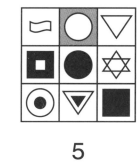 3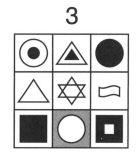

4 5 6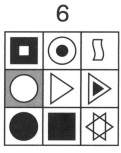

7 8   9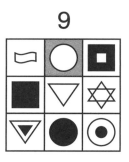

18

What number is missing from the third puzzle?

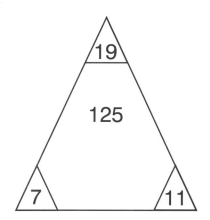

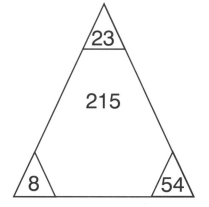

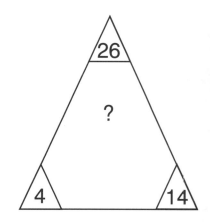

19

Can you work out which letter is missing?

L O T
D H O
P S ?

20

Work out the logic and fill in the missing number.

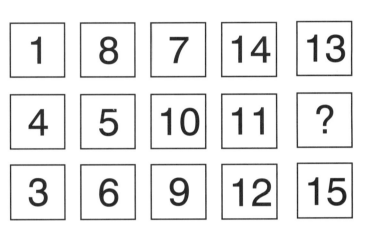

1	8	7	14	13
4	5	10	11	?
3	6	9	12	15

21

Can you work out which letter is missing?

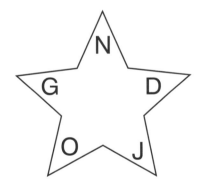

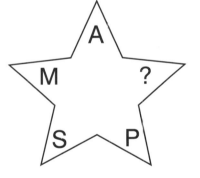

22

Can you work out which numbers are missing?

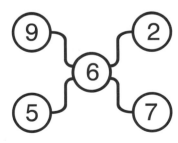

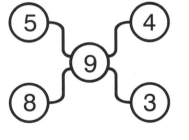

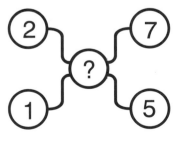

23

Which letter is the odd one out in each of these shapes?

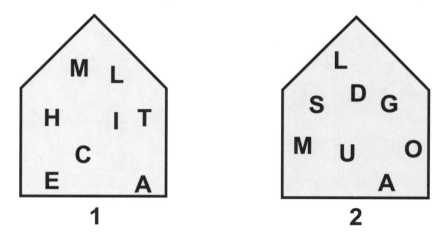

1   2

24

Can you work out what should replace the question mark?

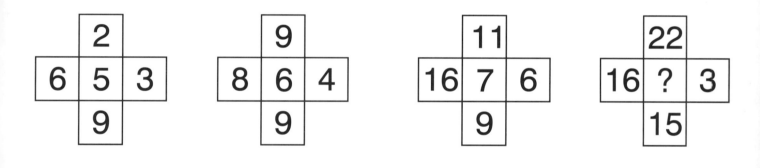

25

Which number replaces the blank?

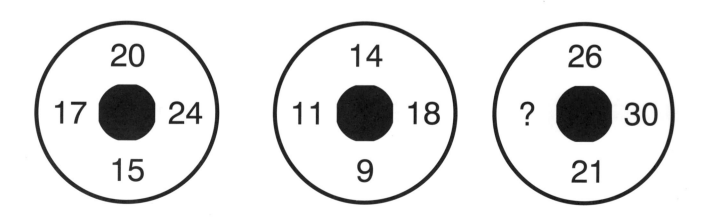

26

By using the same rule for each grid, but without the help of any examples - can you fill in the blanks?

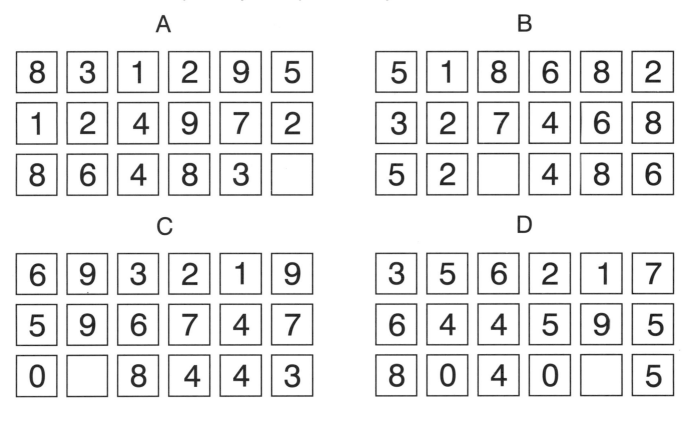

A

8	3	1	2	9	5
1	2	4	9	7	2
8	6	4	8	3	

B

5	1	8	6	8	2
3	2	7	4	6	8
5	2		4	8	6

C

6	9	3	2	1	9
5	9	6	7	4	7
0		8	4	4	3

D

3	5	6	2	1	7
6	4	4	5	9	5
8	0	4	0		5

27

Which hexagon continues the sequence?

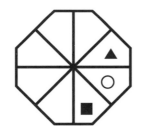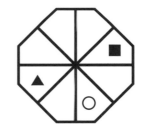

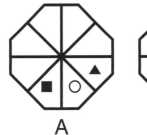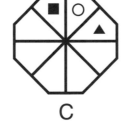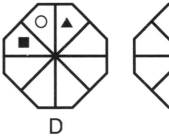

A   B   C   D   E

28

How does this sequence continue?

35
150
305
420
535
650
805
920
1035
1150
1305
1420
?

29

Six books were piled on top of each other on a table. How many moves will it take to move them, one by one on to table C? A book cannot ever be put on top of one smaller than itself.

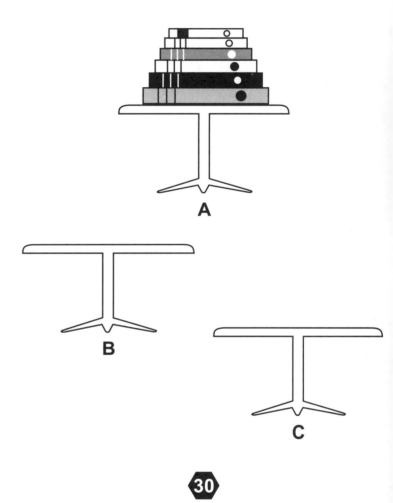

A

B

C

30

Fred dug a hole in four hours. Charlie took six hours to dig a hole the same size, whilst Bill took eight hours.

How long would it take all three men to dig half a hole, assuming that they all worked at the same speed as before and they did not get in each others way?

1

Which letter is missing?

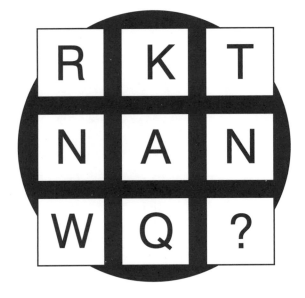

R	K	T
N	A	N
W	Q	?

2

Which letter is missing?

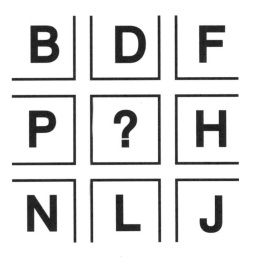

B	D	F
P	?	H
N	L	J

3

Which letter continues this sequence?

A	F	H
K	N	?

T	V	W	X	Z

4

Can you replace the missing letters?

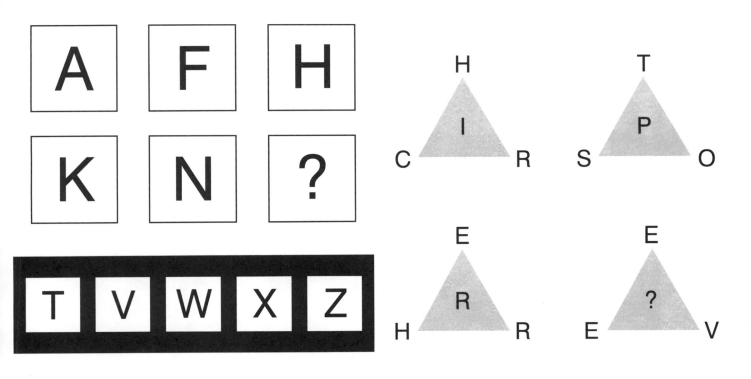

```
    H              T
   I              P
 C     R        S     O

    E              E
   R              ?
 H     R        E     V
```

5

Which of the five numbered pieces goes in the shaded area?

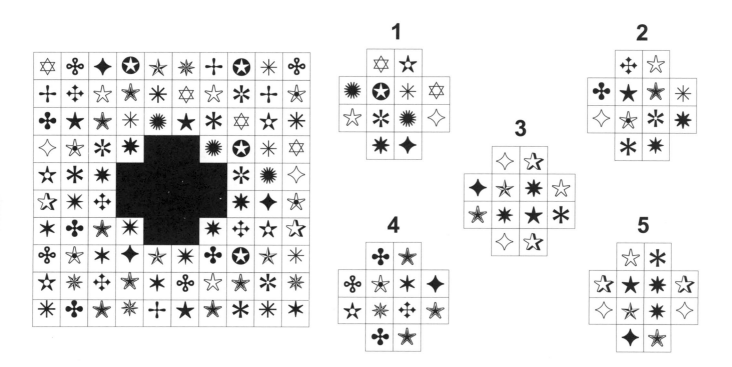

1 **2** **3** **4** **5**

6

Solve this riddle

V is to **Y** as **N** is to

E H T W

7

Which number is missing?

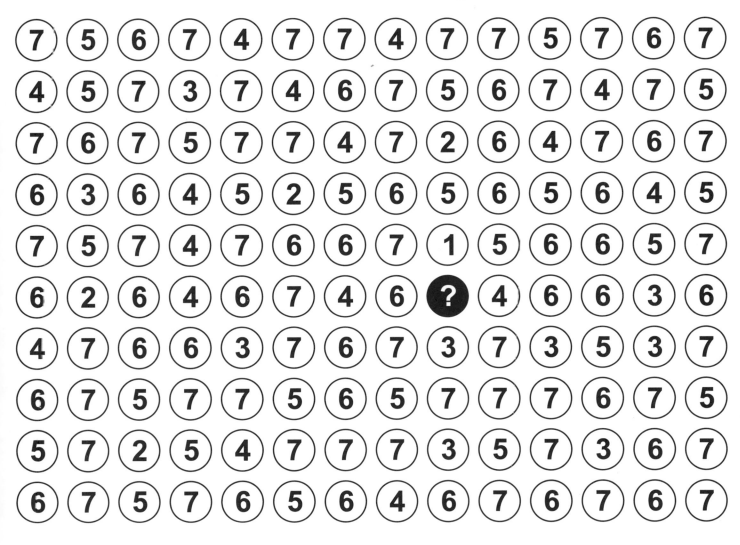

8

Can you work out which letter should replace the blank?

| V | T | Q | M | H | ? |

9

Which flag is the odd one out?

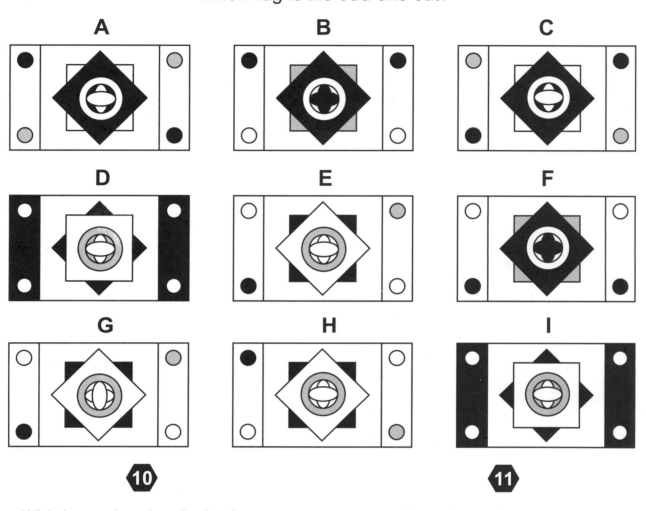

A   B   C

D   E   F

G   H   I

10

Which number is missing?

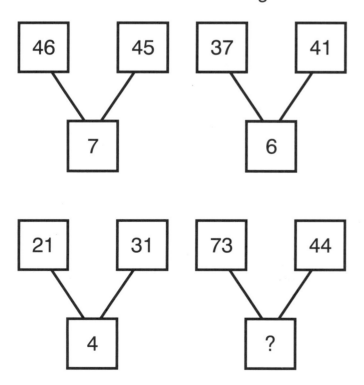

11

Which letter is missing?

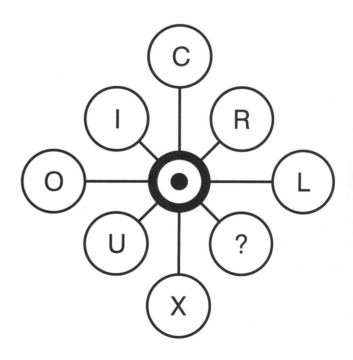

12

Which number goes in the empty square?

4	8	12
9	22	3
11	19	?

2   10   13

15   21   27

13

Which number continues this sequence?

252
124
60
28
12
?

14

Can you fill in the blanks?

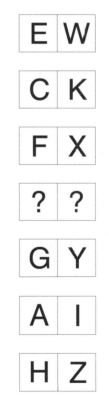

E	W
C	K
F	X
?	?
G	Y
A	I
H	Z

15

Can you insert the missing numbers?
(A different rule applies to each box.)

A

23	20	29
7	6	?

B

42	63	84
18	27	?

C

52	19	28
7	4	?

16

Which letter is the odd one out in each circle?

1

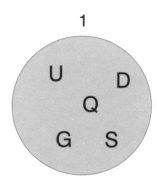

2

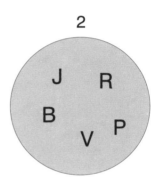

17

Can you fill in the blank?

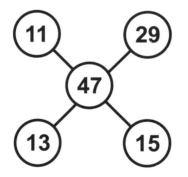

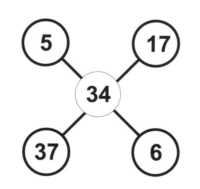

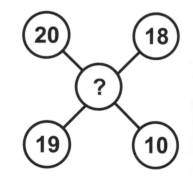

18

What time should the blank clock show?

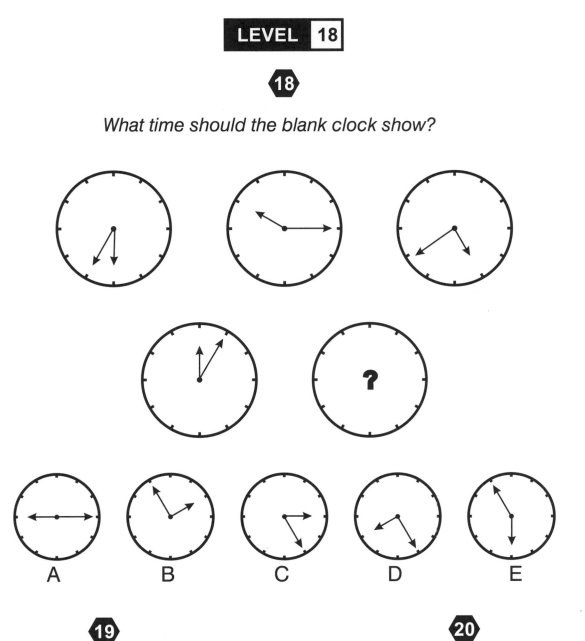

19

Solve this puzzle

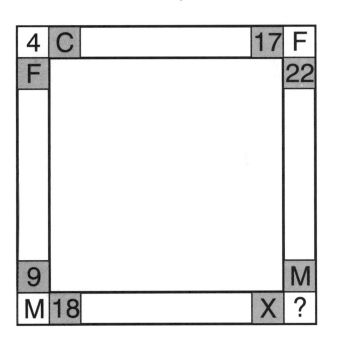

20

Can you complete these puzzles?

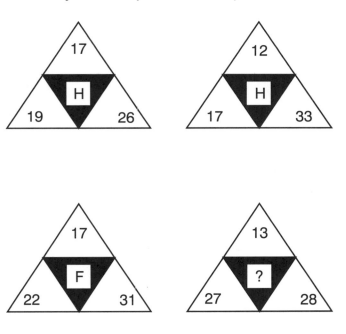

21

Can you replace the question mark?

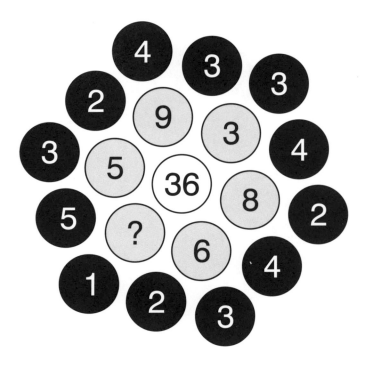

22

Which letter is missing?

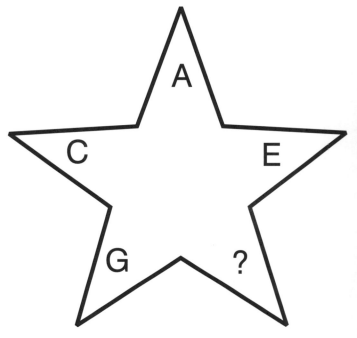

23

Which number replaces the blank and completes the chain?

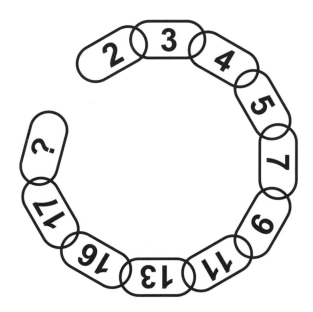

24

Can you replace the missing number?

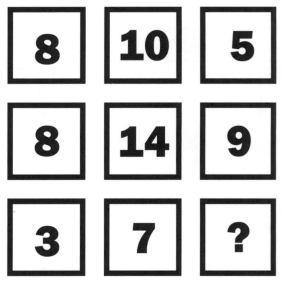

25

Which of the six numbered stars goes in the empty square?

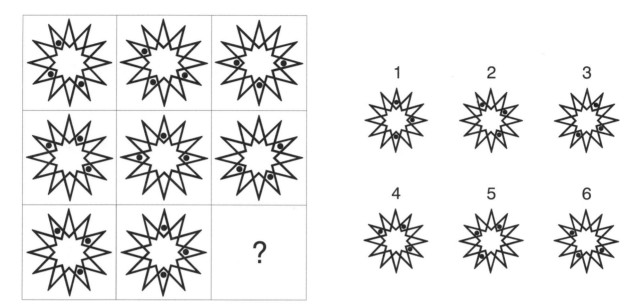

26

Which letter is one up from the letter two up from the letter five down from the letter one up from the letter two up from the letter three up from the letter two down from the letter six down from the top letter?

A

B

C

D

E

F

G

H

27

Which number replaces the blank?

4	?	5
8	■	7
3	9	3

1

Can you insert the missing letter?

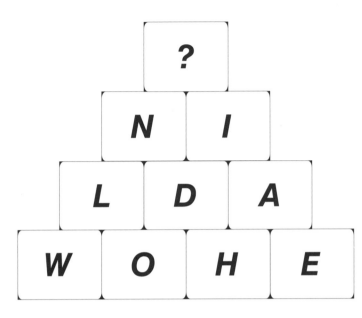

2

Using the numbers and symbols that appear in the top line in every row and column, can you complete this puzzle?

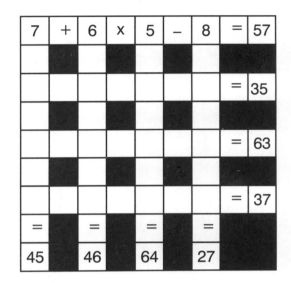

7	+	6	x	5	–	8	=	57
							=	35
							=	63
							=	37
=		=		=		=		
45		46		64		27		

3

Which number replaces the blank and completes the sequence?

6	4	5	3
7	5	4	6
5	?	7	4
8	7	6	5

4

Which of the five numbered pieces goes in the shaded area?

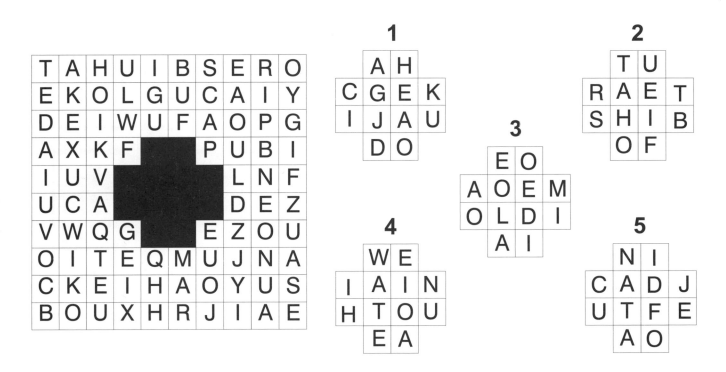

1

```
  A H
C G E K
I J A U
  D O
```

2

```
    T U
R A E T
S H I B
    O F
```

3

```
  E O
A O E M
O L D I
  A I
```

4

```
  W E
I A I N
H T O U
  E A
```

5

```
  N I
C A D J
U T F E
  A O
```

5

Which number completes this sequence?

6

Add the correct number to the empty box.

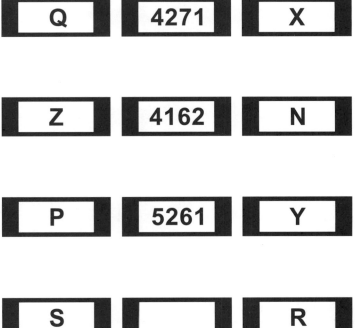

Q	4271	X
Z	4162	N
P	5261	Y
S		R

7

What letter replaces the blank and completes the chain?

8

Can you replace the missing number?

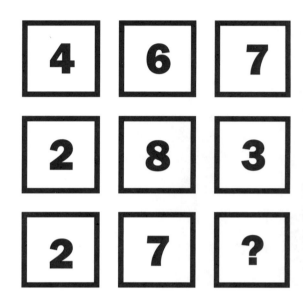

9

Which letter replaces the blank?

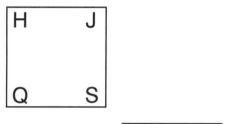

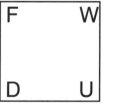

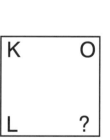

10

Can you complete the sequence?

11

What number is missing from the empty circle?

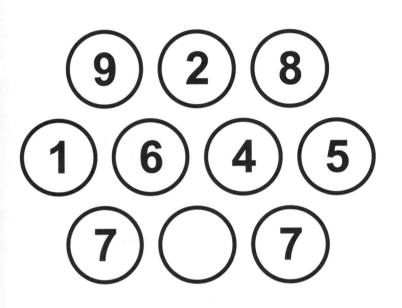

9 2 8

1 6 4 5

7 ◯ 7

12

Complete the last line of this teaser.

1
1 1
2 1
1 1 1 2
3 1 1 2
2 1 1 2 1 3
3 1 2 2 1 3
2 1 2 2 2 3
1 1 4 2 1 3
3 1 1 2 1 3 1 4
? ? ? ? ? ? ? ?

13

Can you replace the missing numbers?

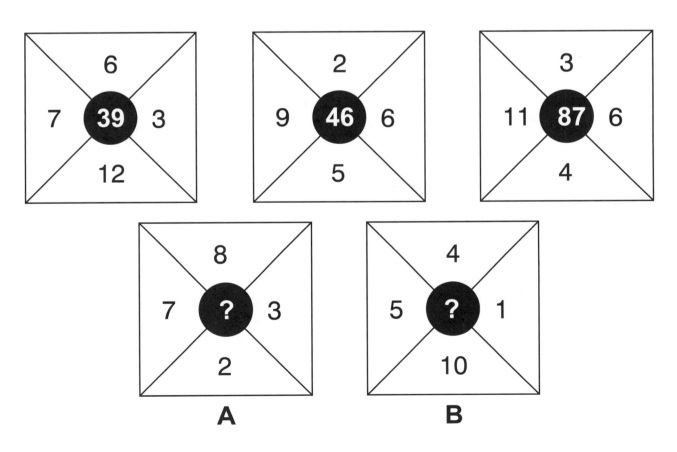

6
7 **39** 3
12

2
9 **46** 6
5

3
11 **87** 6
4

8
7 **?** 3
2

A

4
5 **?** 1
10

B

14

How many squares are in this diagram?

15

What is the missing answer?

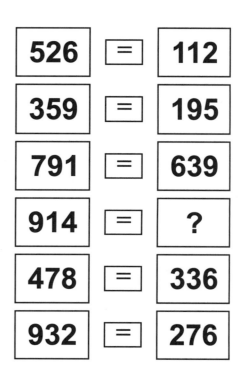

526	=	112
359	=	195
791	=	639
914	=	?
478	=	336
932	=	276

16

Which letter is missing?

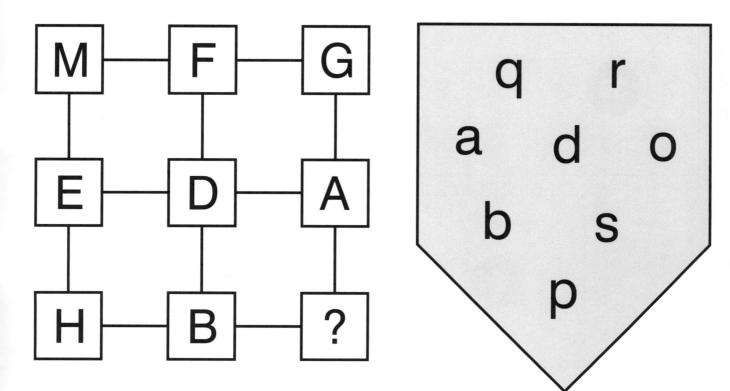

M	F	G
E	D	A
H	B	?

17

Which letter is the odd one out?

q   r

a   d   o

b   s

p

18

Can you fill in the blank?

19

Which square continues the sequence?

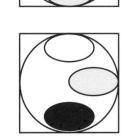
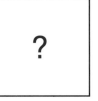
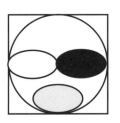

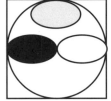
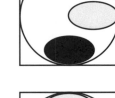
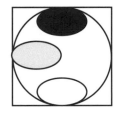

A **B** **C** **D**

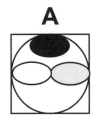
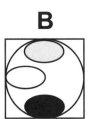
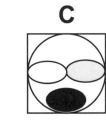
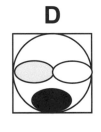

E **F** **G** **H**

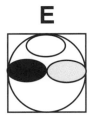

20

Draw three straight lines through the box to end up with six sections, each containing two of each symbol.

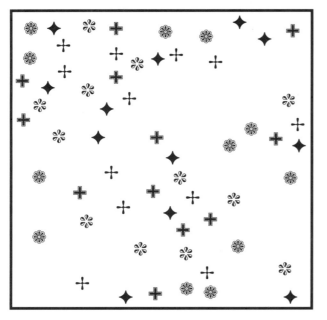

21

Solve this puzzle

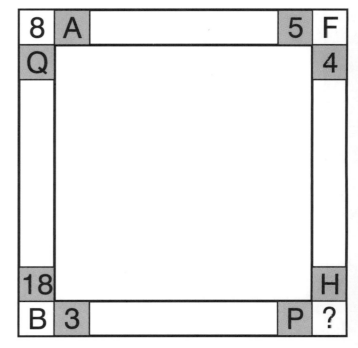

22

Can you work which letter is missing?

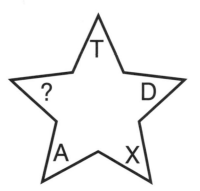

23

Can you work out which number is missing?

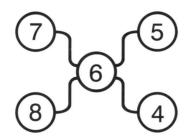

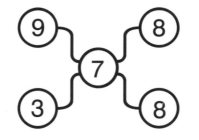

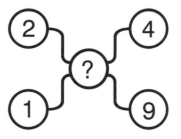

LEVEL 19

24

Which card replaces the blank one?

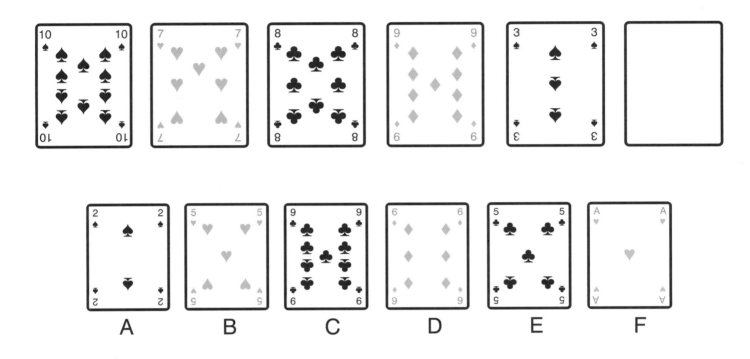

A   B   C   D   E   F

25

Complete this puzzle.

17	13	30	11	19
6	3	9	5	4
23	16	39	16	23
2	11	13	1	
21	5	26	15	11

26

Add one of each of symbol to every box so that no row, column or diagonal of any length contains more than one of each symbol.

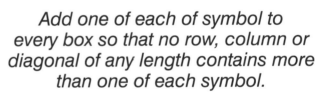

1

Fill in the blank squares - a different rule applies every time.

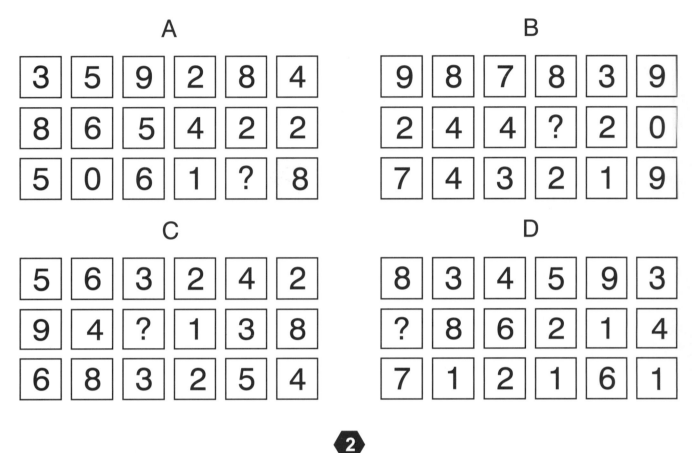

A

3	5	9	2	8	4
8	6	5	4	2	2
5	0	6	1	?	8

B

9	8	7	8	3	9
2	4	4	?	2	0
7	4	3	2	1	9

C

5	6	3	2	4	2
9	4	?	1	3	8
6	8	3	2	5	4

D

8	3	4	5	9	3
?	8	6	2	1	4
7	1	2	1	6	1

2

Which one is the odd one out?

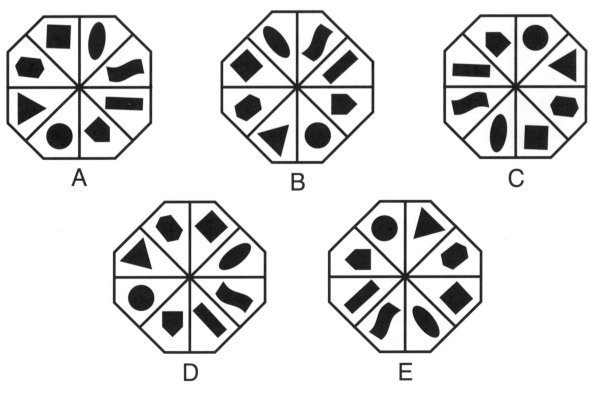

A

B

C

D

E

3

Work out the logic and complete the puzzle.

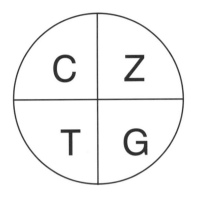

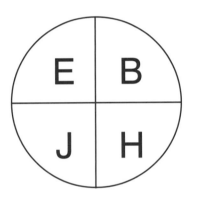

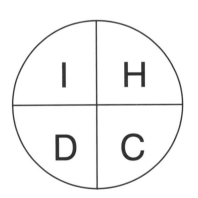

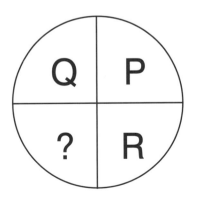

4

Which number is missing?

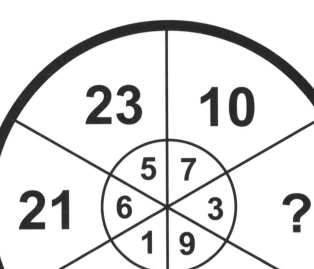

5

Which two digit number completes the puzzle?

Can you replace the question mark?

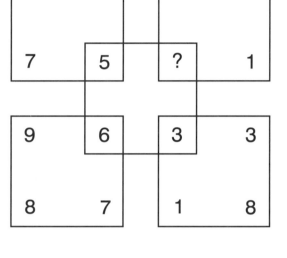

Can you find the missing number?

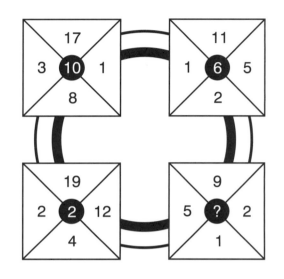

8

Which letter goes in the centre to complete the puzzle?

9

Which letter is missing?

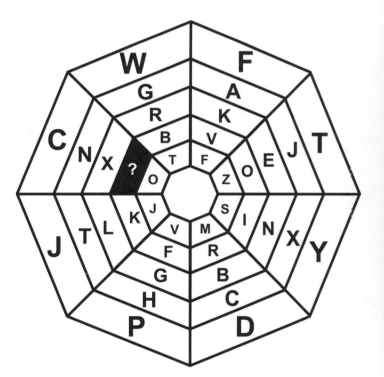

10

Which number continues this sequence?

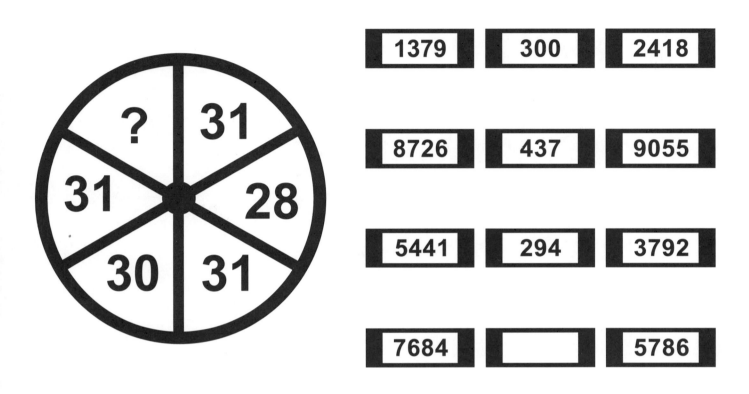

11

Add the correct number to the empty box.

1379	300	2418
8726	437	9055
5441	294	3792
7684		5786

12

Which of the five numbered pieces goes in the shaded area?

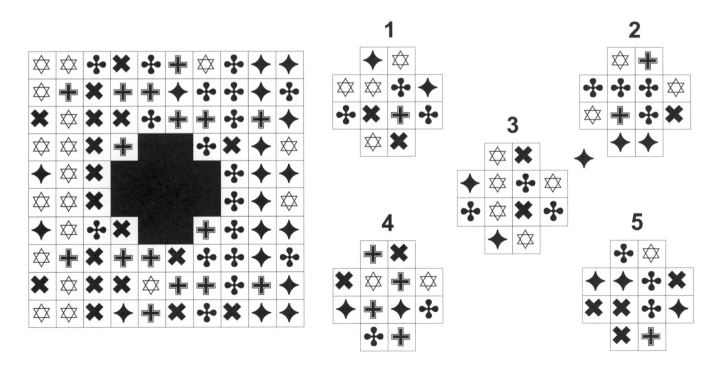

13

Can you replace the missing letter?

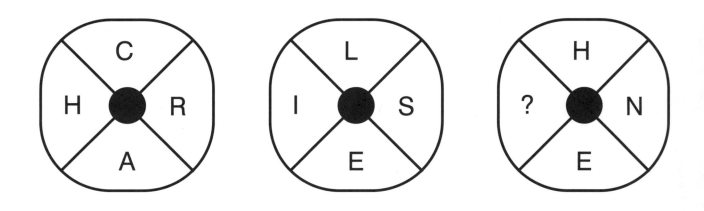

14

Can you work out the logic and solve this puzzle?

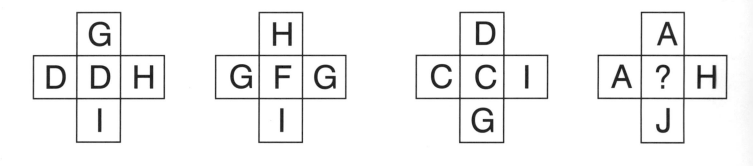

15

Which number replaces the blank?

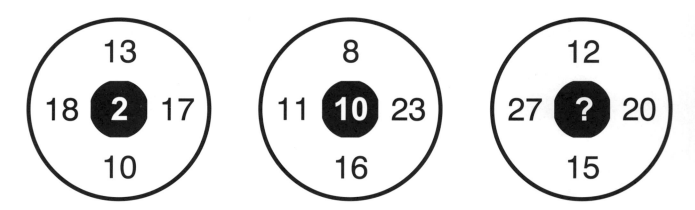

16

Can you fill in the blank?

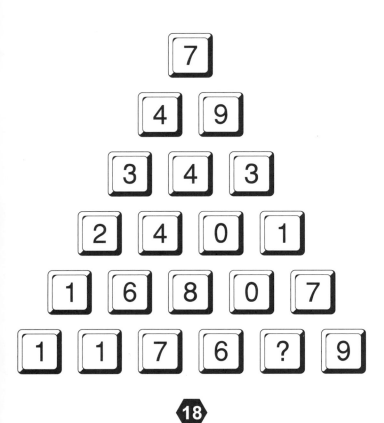

17

Can you complete this number square?

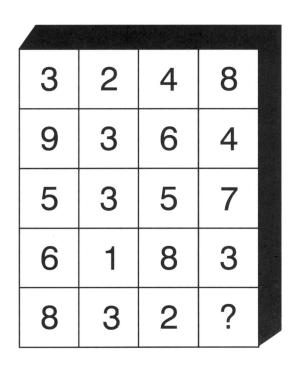

18

Can you fill in the blanks?
(A different rule applies for each puzzle)

19

Study the example puzzles and,
by using the same rule, can you
complete the last puzzle?

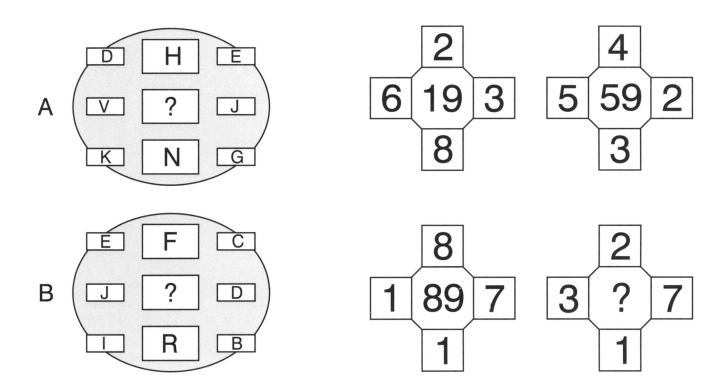

A

B

20

Which square completes the sequence?

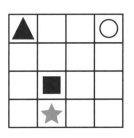
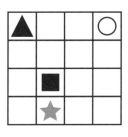
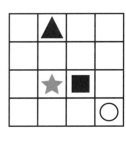
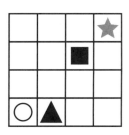

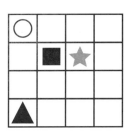
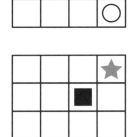
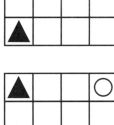
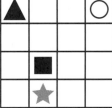

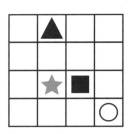
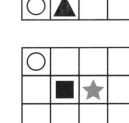
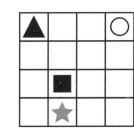
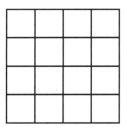

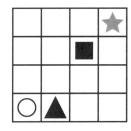
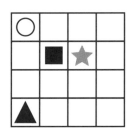
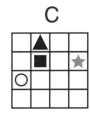
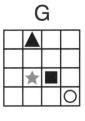

A   B   C   D

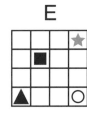
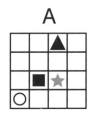
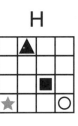

E   F   G   H

1 - 2
Every row and column has got a circle, diamond and square in it. In addition to this, a shape with one, two and three quarters shaded appears in every row and column.

2 - 4
The other numbers are all square numbers of 3, 4, 5 and 6 respectively. Therefore, No 4 will start this sequence, being the square of 2.

3 - E & N
Letters of the alphabet in order zig-zagging downward.

4 - A = 7, B = 13 & C = 12
In Box A the bottom numbers are a third of the top numbers. In Box B the bottom number is 7 less than the top and in Box C the bottom number is half the top one.

5 - 1 = A, 2 = E
These are the only vowels.

6 - A = 7, B = 2
The centre number is the difference between the two numbers at the end of each rod.

7 - 20
Each box is the total of the two boxes directly beneath it.

8

- F
is the only piece with a curve in it.

10 - E
The numbers on the large watch faces add up to 16. Watch E is the only small watch to do this.

11 - S
The letters of the alphabet run from A to Z, missing out two and three letters consecutively.

12 - 28
Twice the total of the numbers around the triangle.

13 - 4
The main grid has got all letters of the alphabet running diagonally from left to right through it, starting in the top left-hand corner, and continuing throughout.

14 - E
The part of the symbol beneath the thick line has been folded onto the top half. The image has then been rotated 45 degrees to the right.

15 - 2
When all the squares in each sum are placed on top of each other they will equal the answer.

16

2S	2S	1W	2E	4W	1S
4S	2S	2E	2W	3W	5W
2E	2E	2S	3S	1N	*
2E	2S	1N	2N	1W	5W
1N	2E	3E	2W	4N	1W
2E	3E	5N	2E	2N	3N

17

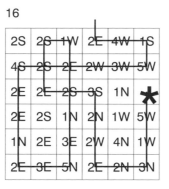

18 - Pig = 4, Cat = 7

19 - A
Starting at the top of the star move one place clockwise adding an extra two letters each time:
C (DE) F (GHIJ) K (LMNOPQ) R (STUVWXYZ) A.

20 - 1
The difference between the sum of the top row and the sum of the bottom row.

21 - 3
The last symbol in each column and row is always the same as the preceding two symbols minus any part which has been duplicated.

22 - C
Keep adding up the figures until a single digit is reached.
eg A = 9 (2 + 9 + 4 + 3 = 18, 1 + 8 = 9)

23 - 14
The bottom figure is one quarter the combined total of the top numbers.

24 - A = 12, B = 3 & C = 30
The number on the right-hand side of the circle is three times greater than that on the left.

25 - A = 49, B = 26
All the other numbers can be divided by 3.

26 - A
The symbols are upside-down mirror images of the numbers 1 -5. Symbol A is the upside-down mirror image of No 6.

27 -1
Each row and column contains the following features: Black hair, white hair and grey hair; a black T-shirt, a white T-shirt and a grey T-shirt; a black beaker, a white beaker and a grey beaker.

28 1 = N, 2 = N & 3 = B
The letters on the right-hand side of each circle are four places in front of the letters in the opposite segments.

1 - 4
Starting in the top left segment. Move clockwise taking away 6 to get the second number, dividing this by 3 for the third and multiplying this by 4 to finish.

2 - J
Starting at A and moving clockwise, the letters increase by 3 each step.

3 -90
The centre number is the total when you multiply each connecting line.

4 - 2
Each column adds up to 16.

5 - J
Go forward four letters then back one and repeat until the end.

6 - Z
The letters on the left of the circle are five in front of those in the opposite segments.

7 - 624
The centre box is four times the difference between the other two numbers in each row.

8 - 2
Each of the shapes in the bottom squares are exact opposites of the top squares. e.g. on the top row there is a large ellipse with a small square inside; the bottom row shows this as a large square with a small ellipse inside. The missing shape is therefore a large circle with a small triangle inside.

9 - D
The letters at the top of each triangle increase by 3 each step, the letters in the bottom left increase by 4, and those in the bottom right increase by 5.

10 - 2
Add the first two columns and subtract the third to give the total in the fourth column.

11 - Y
Move the same number of letters from the second to the third rows and columns as you have from the first to the second.

LEVEL 2

12 - 6
It is the only one where the large grey circle and the large white circle are in the same sector. Each of the other shapes have just been rotated slightly.

13 - A = 18 & B = 30
Multiply each of the inner numbers and add together all of the outer ones. The answer will be the same and this is what should go in the centre.

14 - 0
The bottom number is double the top number, minus 1 for the first box, 2 for the second, etc. The final number is 3 x 2 - 6 = 0

15 - D
Each third row or column shows the symbols which have been repeated in the same position in the preceding two pictures.

16 - 1
The total of the top row in each box is the same as the total of the bottom row.

17 - 22
Add up all the digits in the square: (3 + 7) + (2 + 1) + (1 + 5) + (1 + 2) = 22

18 - 3
The number of small black squares increases by two each column and by one each row.

19 - A
The shapes undulate with each step as well as following a colour pattern - black, grey, white. Shape A is the only white shape smaller than the last piece.

20 - C
A = 1, B = 2 etc. Take away the second column or row from the first.

21 - 49
The opposite numbers are all squares of each other; the square of 7 is 49.

22 - D
There are two series of letters, vowels and consonants. Both increase by one as they alternate along the chain.

23 - 23
Add the first and last numbers in each row and column to find the centre number each time.

24 - W
Top left letters increase by one, top right decrease by two, bottom left decrease by one and bottom right increase by two.

25 - 54
Alternate between adding 3 and multiplying by 3 each step.
2 (+3) 5 (x3) 15 (+3) 18 (x3) 54 (+3) 57

26 - F

27 - 97
Each number is twice the preceding one, minus 1.
(49 x 2) - 1 = 97

28 - Z
A = 1, B = 2 etc. Add up the smaller ellipses and enter the answer (as a letter) in the larger ellipse.

LEVEL 3

1 - B

2 - A
Each block of four squares moves 45 degrees anti-clockwise each step. The symbols on the outside however move 45 degrees clockwise each time.

3 - He was in his uniform.

4 - P
Each square contains the letter that is midway between the linking boxes.

5 -
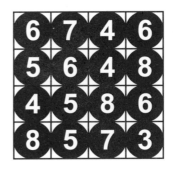

6 - 3
The number of straight lines needed to write the numbers in Roman numerals.

7 - O
Miss out three letters as you move from column to column and one letter from row to row.

8
Multiply the figures given and add the digits of the answer together to get a single figure number.
e.g. (7 x 6 x 3 = 126) 1 + 2 + 6 = 9

9 - A = 6, B = 4
Both halves of each circle add up to the same figure.

10 -

The letters in the top row decrease by three each step whilst those in the bottom row increase by two.

11 - E
The cards alternate between red and black each step. They also increase by four when it goes from a red card to a black one and decrease by three when it goes from black to red.

12 - V
The letters go up by three each time, moving from the top to bottom of each tile before moving on to the next one.

13 - 7
Add the second column to the first and divide by the third to reach the figure in the fourth.

14 - A = 35, B = 15
Divide the smaller boxes in each line by three then multiply them together to get the centre figure.

15 - Q
A = 1, B = 2 etc.
C x E - B + D = Q
(3 x 5 - 2 + 4 = 17)

16 - I
A & F are reverse images of each other, as are D & E, C & H and B & G.

17 - 9
Add 4 + 5 and 6 + 3, in both cases the answer will be the same.

18 - R
Each letter is three places away from its opposite letter.

19 - 1 = F, 2 = F
Starting in the top section, move clockwise around the square, missing out three letters each step.

20 - A = 18, B = 10 & C = 18
e.g. A = (6 + 5) + (9 - 2) = 18

LEVEL 3

21 - N
The centre letter is midway between the other letters connected by the line.

22 - 59
Start in the top corner and move clockwise. Add the first two numbers (8 + 7 = 15) to the second number (15 + 7 = 22), then add the first three numbers (8 + 7 + 22 = 59) to get the solution.

23 - G
The centre letter is midway between the letters diagonally opposite each other.

24 - B
Take away the number of objects in the second columns and rows from the first to get the third.

25 - 16
The numbers in each ellipse add up to 100.

26 - C
The bottom letters are 4,6,8 and 10 letters in front of the top letters.

27 - F
Each block contains features which appear in both blocks directly beneath it.

28 - D
The hour hand is pointing to a number that is double what the minute hand is pointing to.

29 - 1 = O, 2 = V & 3 = U
A = 1, B = 2 etc.
Add up the numbers in each column and place the answer, in the form of a letter, in the centre box.

30 - A = 8, B = 12 & C = 6
The centre figure is double the difference between the total of the numbers on the bottom and the number at the top of each triangle.

LEVEL 4

1 - 6
Add the number of partitioned areas in the first and third columns to get the total in the second.

2 - 22
The difference between each number increases by an extra one each step.

3 - H & R
The first square increases by three letters each step and the second by four.

4 - A = 4, B = 10, C = 3 & D = 9
Divide the top number by three and add two to get the bottom number.

5 - 1 = R, 2 = J
All other letters are drawn using straight lines only.

6 - A = 8, B = 3
Take the total of the top row away from the total of the bottom.

7 - 57
Each box is the total of the two boxes directly beneath it, plus two.

8 -

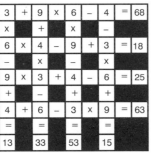

9 -

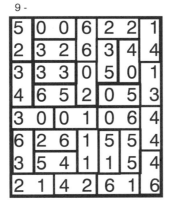

10 - B
The figures shown as hours are one quarter the total of the figures shown as minutes.

11 - X
Move forward an extra five places each time.

12 - A = 1, B = 5, C = 3 & D = 4
Multiply the top number by the bottom left and divide that answer by the bottom right.

13 - 4
Go through the alphabet, returning to A when Z is reached, in two directions. First from the top left square, move diagonally from left to right every other row. Then fill in the blank squares moving from top to bottom, left to right.

14 - F
Rotated ninety degrees then turned upside down.

15 -

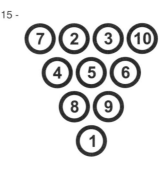

16 - Use Roman numerals.
IXXX - I = XXX

17 -

18 -

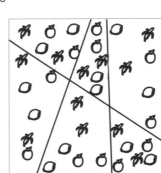

19 -

20 - 1 = L, 2 = T
Start at the top of the star and move clockwise. Add three letters on the first move, then subtract one, then repeat this again.

21 - A = 5, B = 7
Apart from the number 1, the centre figure is the only number that the others can all be divided by.

22 - 3
Add the features from the second column to the first, then take away the features in the third.

23 - E
Add up the first two digits of the first column to get the first two digits of the second. Then do the same again for the next two digits.
E = 1313, (4+9) & (9+4) = (13) (13)

24 = A = 10, B = 8
The square root of the total of the top two numbers.

25 - A = 10, B = 13
Starting with the lowest number, move clockwise, adding an extra 2 each step.

26 - 1 = b, 2 = v
When written in lower case the letters in box 1, except b, do not have any descenders or risers. The opposite is true in box 2.

27

(maple leaf) = 6   (person) = 7
(lightbulb) = 4   (gear/flower) = 5

28

13	3	2	16
8	10	11	5
12	6	7	9
1	15	14	4

LEVEL 5

1 - 5

2 - Bob = A, Bill = B, Barry = C, Brian = D and Bernie = E

3 - A = 4, B = 28
Start in the top left corner and move clockwise. Multiply the first number by itself, then add five and, finally, double it.

4 - Y
Move forward 10 places each step, returning to A whenever Z is reached.

5 - 8
Multiply or divide each pair of numbers joined by the line.

6 - A = 2, B = 20
Start in the top left corner and move clockwise. Add five to the first number, divide this by four and multiply this answer by five.

7 -

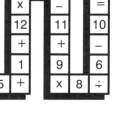

= 7   = 8

= 10   = 9

8 -

7		3	−	4		66
+		x		−		=
13		12		11		10
x		+		+		−
2		1		9		6
÷	5	+		x	8	÷

9 - 7

10 - O
1st consonant, 1st vowel, 2nd consonant, 2nd vowel, etc. etc.

11 - 30
The total of every digit in the left and right boxes.

12 - 3
The number of sides on each shape increases by one every step.

13 -

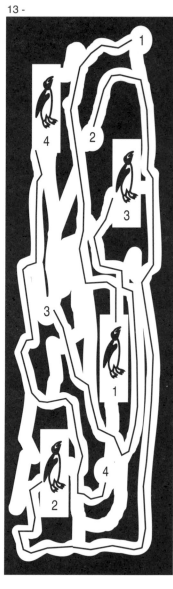

14 - 17
The numbers in each row increase by 4, 5 & 6 respectively.

15 - C = 1, K = 2, J = 3, B = 4, A = 5, 6 = D, 7 = G, 8 = E, 9 = H, 0 = F

16 -

13
1

The top line from left to right contains all the prime numbers. The bottom right from right to left contains square numbers.

17 - B
Move from left to right, top to bottom. One of the eight segments disappears every other step whilst the black dot moves one place anti-clockwise every step.

18 - 0
Each pair of diagonally opposite numbers add up to the same total.

19 - A = 4, B = 14 & C = 20
Double the difference between the total of the top and bottom numbers and the left and right numbers.

20 -
Alan (3) & Anne (5), Andrew (1) & Alison (6), Anthony (4) & Andrea (7), Arthur (2) & Angela (8)

21 - 5
The letters of the alphabet (T - Y) turned on their side and mirrored.

22 - V
The steps between each column and row increase by the position in the alphabet of the letter. eg K is the 11th letter so move forward 11 spaces.

23 - 12
60 seconds in a minute, 60 minutes in an hour, 24 hours in a day, 7 days in a week, 4 weeks in a month and 12 months in a year.

24 - O
Only letters containing curved lines are used.

25 - 2
Add the first and third columns and rows together and then add these digits together to get a single number.
e.g. 8 + 2 = 10, 1 + 0 = 1

26 - 1 = O, 2 = Y
Start in the top right corner and move anti-clockwise. Go forward five spaces for the first letter, back one for the next and forward a further six for the last one.

27 - 48
The six highest numbers that can be scored with a single dart. 60 (Treble 20), 57 (Treble 19), 54 (Treble 18), 51 (Treble 17), 50 (Bullseye) and 48 (Treble 16).

LEVEL 6

1 - A = 10, B = 14
Subtract the inner numbers from the outer numbers. Add up the difference from each corner and write this amount in the centre.

2 - 1 = L & R, 2 = E & N, 3 = C & U
Start in the top left corner, move down the first column, up the second, down the third etc. through the alphabet.

3 - A = 33, B = 49
Start at the lowest number and move clockwise adding an extra three each step.

4 - None
Bread goes in a toaster!

5 -

$53 + 27 - 30 + 18 = 68$

Move one line from the first 9 to make it a 5, add this to the 16 to make it 18.

6 -   One solution is:

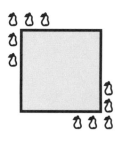

7 - 8
Every row, column and diagonal will add up to 21.

8 - F
The alphabet in reverse is replaced by numbers. i.e. Z = 1, Y = 2 etc. Add the first and third letters from each row and column and put the answer in the centre square.

9 - 40
Add together the corner squares of each row and column and put the answer in the next middle square going in a clockwise direction.

10 - 1 = P, 2 = Z & 3 = T
A = 1, B = 2 etc.
Add up the letters around each triangle and write the answer, in the form of a letter, in the centre.

LEVEL 6

11 - A = 8, B = 8, C = 7 & D = 0
Add up each column and carry over the tens to the next column.

12 - C
One half of the hexagon is reversed each step. Top half, bottom half, left half and finally the right half.

13 - E
Red cards are all odd numbers and increase alternately with the decreasing black cards which are all even numbers.

14 -

21	4	15	24	1
6	8	17	14	20
3	19	13	7	23
10	12	9	18	16
25	22	11	2	5

15 -

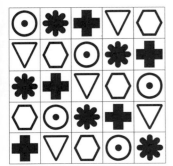

16 - 9
It is the only piece which has more sides on the inner shape than the outer one.

17 - A = 10, B = 16 & C = 14
Add up all the digits in the top boxes.

18 - T
A = 1, B = 2 etc.
Each pair of letters, joined by a straight line, adds up to 25.

19 - 1 = W, 2 = F
Start in the top section and move clockwise 10 places each time, returning to A whenever Z is reached.

20
A = 10, B = 7 & C = 3
Add up the top three numbers and divide the total by the bottom number.

21 - 21
(11 x 9) - (6 x 13) = 21

22 -

P	A	Z	T	Q	C
A	R	B	H	J	A
Z	B	T	A	V	Y
T	H	A	X	D	M
Q	J	V	D	O	E
C	A	Y	M	E	N

The grid reads the same across as down.

23 - 5
The total of each segment on the bottom half is one less than the total in the opposite segment in the top half.

24 -
1 = Paul, 2 = Peter, 3 = Patrick, 4 = Phillip, 5 = Percy.

25 - 47
Using prime numbers:
A = 2, B = 3, C = 5,
D = 7, E = 11, F = 13,
G = 17.

26 - E
Each box contains only the elements that have been duplicated in the two boxes directly beneath it. However the boxes are turned upside down on each layer.

27 - C
When written in hours in minutes (i.e. 3.45, 6.15, 8.40 etc) the digits will add up to twelve.

28 - Cows cannot talk!

29 -
A = 12 x 5 ÷ 10 = 6
B = 3 x 8 ÷ 2 = 12
C = 6 x 9 ÷ 3 = 18

LEVEL 7

1 - 4
Add the dots that appear in the first two rows and columns to the third, except: when two white circles are carried over change it to black and two black ones should be changed to white.

2 - F

3 - 20
The total of the first two rows and columns minus one.

4 - A = 1, B = 5, C = 1 & D = 6
The difference between the first and second numbers in each row divided by two.

5 - 1 = H & 2 = C
Place all the letters in each circle in alphabetical order and they will form a chain of letters, each time missing out two.
e.g. A..D..G..J..M..P

6 - A = 6 & B = 5
Multiply the numbers on the top row. Then add the numbers together on the bottom row. The centre figure is the difference between these figures.
e.g. (8 x 4 = 32) (19 + 7 = 26) = 6

7 - 168
The number in each box is the multiplied total of the two boxes directly beneath it.

8 -

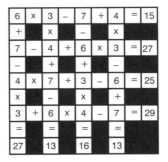

9 -

1	4	3	6	3	2	5
4	4	2	6	4	3	0
1	0	1	4	3	5	5
5	1	5	6	3	2	3
0	3	5	0	0	4	5
4	5	6	0	0	3	2
1	6	6	2	1	1	4
2	2	6	1	2	0	6

10 - B
Add the digits shown as minutes together to match the figure shown as hours.

11 - Q
Go forward ten letters, back five and keep repeating.

12 - A = 26, B = 24 & C = 33
Start at the lowest number and move anti-clockwise adding the same number each time. The number in the centre is the next logical one.

13 - 4
Two chains of letters on alternate diagonal rows, both starting in the top right corner and moving from left to right. The first chain contains every letter of the alphabet, the second contains every letter except vowels.

14 -
A = Claire - 1st
B = Carl - 2nd
C = Chris - 3rd
D = Carol - 4th

15 - 4

16 -

17	24	1	8	15
23	5	7	14	16
4	6	13	20	22
10	12	19	21	3
11	18	25	2	9

17 -

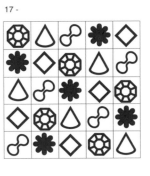

- 199 -

SOLUTIONS ~ SOLUTIONS ~ SOLUTIONS ~ SOLUTIONS ~ SOLUTIONS

LEVEL 7

18 - J
A = 1, B = 2 etc
Add the two numbers of each line and write the answer, as a letter, in the centre box opposite.

19 - 13
Multiply the top and bottom numbers and write your answers in a straight row beneath the box: 1 2 3 4 5 6 7 8 9 10

20 - 1 = D & 2 = S
Starting at the top of the star and moving clockwise, go forward five letters, then back three and keep repeating.

21 - A = 5 & B = 14
(16 ÷ 4) + (15 - 5) = 14

22 - 4
Start in the top left corner and move clockwise in a spiral pattern towards the centre. Add one petal each step and one leaf every other step.

23 - E
The second column is the number required to bring the total of each line up to 10,000.

24 - A = 11 & B = 15
Add up all the digits in the top part of the circle.
A = 1 + 4 + 3 + 3 = 11

25 - A = 14 & B = 16
Multiply the digits in each of the left-hand segments to get the answer opposite.
A = 2 x 7 = 14, 3 x 4 = 12 etc.

26 - 1 = N & 2 = Q
A = 1, B = 2 etc.
All other letters are divisable by 4 (Box 1) or 3 (Box 2).

27 - Joe - £540, John - £270 and Jamie £90.

28 -

16	11	12
9	13	17
14	15	10

LEVEL 8

1 - 2 & 5

2 -
A - 5 x 2 + 4 ÷ 2 - 1 = 6
B - 8 - 2 ÷ 3 x 4 + 1 = 9
C - 9 ÷ 3 x 4 - 8 + 7 = 11

3 - V
Each diagonally opposite pair of letters is the same number of spaces in from the start and finish of the alphabet.
e.g. L is the 12th letter from the beginning, O is the 12th letter from the end.

4 - -6
The square of the number in the smaller circle, minus multiples of 5.
(1 x 1) -5, (2 x 2) - 10 etc.

5 - 18
The difference between each pair of numbers.

6 - 10
Add up all the digits in each pair of numbers.

7 - 10
Each number indicates the position in the alphabet of the previous letter.

8 - 15
Moving in a clockwise direction, two chains of numbers in alternate segments, 3, 6, 9, 12 and 5, 10, 15, 20.

9 - A = XX & B = XV
Add up the numbers around the triangle and write the answer, in Roman Numerals, in the box.

10 - T
All the others read the same upside down.

11 - 6
Add the two outside columns together and then add the digits of this answer together.
e.g. 1424 + 4937 = 6361,
6 + 3 + 6 + 1 = 16

12 - 4
The grey segment moves anti-clockwise one place each step, the circle moves one place clockwise, whilst the square alternates between top and bottom.

13 - 9
1 & 5 are the same, as are 2 & 8, 3 & 4 and 6 & 7.

14 - 9
In each row and column, three numbers add up to the fourth.

15 -

5	10	3
4	6	8
9	2	7

16 -

9
17

There are two chains of numbers: A range of prime numbers, from 7 to 23 running in a zig-zag pattern from left to right, and a range of square numbers, from 1 to 36, in the empty squares from right to left.

17 - D
Moving in a spiral pattern from the top left corner and finishing at the centre square; the black square moves clockwise 2 spaces, then 3, then 4 etc. etc. The circle moves anti-clockwise around the four inner squares.

18 - 12
Add up the three numbers in each square and divide it by two. Write this answer in the other square.

19 - A = 22, B = 30 & C = 35
Starting at the lowest number in each square, move clockwise adding an extra number each step. The centre figure is the next logical number to appear.

20 - L
Start in the top left corner and move down from left to right. Miss out one letter in the first column, two in the second and so on.

21 - 13
A = 1, B = 2 etc
Both halves add up to 100.

22 - P
There are two chains of letters, one starting at each end of the line and each one using every fourth letter of the alphabet in alternate squares.

23 - A = 7 & B = 4
Start at the highest number and divide by 5, 4, 3 and 2 in turn.

24 - 187
Add the two preceding numbers together and take away one.

25 - J
Start in the top left corner and move in a spiral pattern towards the centre, missing out alternate letters.

26 -

P	D	K	R	S
D	A	Z	Y	E
K	Z	U	B	C
R	Y	B	J	T
S	E	C	T	H

The grid reads the same across as it does down.

27 - 11
The mid-way point between pairs of corner numbers is placed in the centre square of the following line in a clockwise direction.

28 - A = 24 & B = 5
Start at the lowest number and move clockwise, doubling it and taking away 1, then 2, then 3 each step.

29 - r
A chain of letters, which, when written in lower case, do not have descenders or risers.

30 - 4
The total of the four corner squares and the total of the four middle squares is written in the centre.

LEVEL 9

LEVEL 10

1 - A = 12 (Divide the top number by two and add three)
B = 33 (Double the top number and take away five)
C = 40 (Multiply by three and take away two)

2 - 1 = M & 2 = E
All other letters are made up of three straight lines.

3 - A = 23 & B = 25
Add up all the digits in the four outer circles.

4 - E
The times will read the same when the watches are turned upside down.

5 - P
Every letter of the alphabet that is made using both straight lines and curves.

6 - 9
Take away the totals in the bottom triangles from the totals in the top triangles.

7 - A = 14 & B = 8
Start at the lowest number and move anti-clockwise. Add three for the next number, double this and add two for the next and finally add the first number to get the last one.

8 - K
A = 1, B = 2 etc
The first six prime numbers.

9 - 60
Multiply each pair of numbers.

10 - 10
Each diagonal line adds up to 30.

11 - O
The letters all read the same upside down.

12
A = 2 of Clubs, B = 3 of Diamonds, C = 6 of Spades, D = 7 of Spades, E = 4 of Hearts, F = 10 of Clubs and G = 2 of Clubs.

Each of the end cards of every row denotes the total value of the other cards.
e.g. A 4 of Hearts indicates that the red cards in that row are all Hearts and that they will add up to 4.

13 - E
The bottom letter is the same number of spaces in from the end of the alphabet as the top letter is from the start.

14 - 8
The largest number in each row and column is the total of all the other numbers which appear in that line.

15 - A = 30 & B = 30
The total of the two corner numbers is written in the middle box of the following line, moving in a clockwise direction. The centre box is the total of all the digits in the four middle boxes.

16 - R
A = 1, B = 2 etc
Add up the letters around the outside and write the answer, as a letter, in the centre.

17 - C
Give each small box a number between 1 and 16, starting in the top left corner and moving left to right, top to bottom.

Add the value of the black squares in each of the first two columns and rows and transfer this answer to the third line.

Take away the value of the circle in the second rows and columns from the first and transfer this answer to the third line.

Finally, add the value of the black square and white circle in each box and enter a triangle in the correct square, starting back at the first box whenever the end is reached.

18 - The other half are girls as well.

19 -

20 - 16
A = 1, B = 2 etc.
The value of the letters squared, minus twenty.
e.g. F = 6 x 6 = 36 - 20 = 16

21 - 96
Add the first and third rows and columns, double this answer and transfer it to the middle box.

22 - C
Write the figures as Roman Numerals. The answer is the number of straight lines needed to do this.

23 - 1 = F, 2 = B & 3 = A
A = 1, B = 2 etc.
Add the bottom row to the top and write the answer in the middle row.

24 - A = 22, B = 26 & C = 15
Multiply the bottom two numbers and add the answer to the top number to reach the centre figure.

25 - 1 = T & 2 = B
Start at the top letter and move anti-clockwise. Move forward 2 letters, then 12, then 22 and then 32.

26 - A = 2 & B = 4
Multiply each diagonal line and double the difference.

27 - A = 11 & B = 9
The difference between each pair of numbers at the three points of the triangle.

28 - 1 = C & L, 2 = H & Q and 3 = D & M
A chain of letters in alphabetical order, starting in the top left square and moving from left to right in a diagonal pattern.

29 - A = 25 & B = 1
Z = 1, Y = 2 etc.
Each number indicates the position of the alphabet, in reverse, of the opposite letter.

1 - 3
The sequence is made up of two clockwise spirals, one starting in the top left corner and the other starting in the first available square in the bottom right corner.

2 - 4
Multiply each pair of opposite numbers and get the same number.

3 - 654
Add up the first three boxes from each column. The bottom row will read 987654321.

4 - A = 3, B = 4, C = 3 & D =3
Add the second row to the first and multiply by the third to get the same answer for each column.

5 - B
The black square moves clockwise two segments each step, the white circle moves three segments anti-clockwise each step whilst the black triangle alternates between two opposite segments.

6 - 1 = R & 2 = L
Start in the top quarter and move in a clockwise direction the same number of letters each step.

7 - A = 8, B = 2 & C = 2
Add up all the outer numbers and then add up the digits from this answer so that a single figure is reached.
A = (9 + 7 + 2 + 8 = 26) 2 + 6 = 8

8 - 4
The difference between the total of the odd numbers and the even numbers.

9 - C
The clock moves forward 100 minutes each step.

10 - She is 30 and her niece and nephew 10.

11 - A = 21, B = 12 & C = 20
Multiply the bottom two numbers and take away the top number.

SOLUTIONS ~ SOLUTIONS ~ SOLUTIONS ~ SOLUTIONS ~ SOLUTIONS ~ SOLUTIONS

LEVEL 10

12 - 5
Start in the top left corner and move anti-clockwise in a spiral pattern towards the centre. The white circle alternates between two opposite points whilst the black circle moves one step anti-clockwise each step.

13 - D

14 - 4
Two numbers from each row and column add up to the third.

15 - 9
Each line of blocks will total 19.

16 -

9	+	5	x	2	−	3	=	25
+		+		x		+		
2	+	9	−	3	x	5	=	40
−		x		+		−		
5	−	3	x	9	+	2	=	20
x		−		−		x		
3	+	2	x	5	−	9	=	16
=		=		=		=		
18		40		10		54		

17 - 8
Each block of any four will total 17.

18 - J
Move forward one letter, then two, then three and keep repeating this sequence until the end.

19 - 9
Add the first and third columns and rows and take away two for the middle number.

20 - 1 = D & 2 = C
A = 1, B = 2 etc.
When all the letters are added up in each box they will total 26.

21 - 30
The number of days in each of the first 6 months.

LEVEL 11

1 - 5
Every row and column contains a plant of each design in each of three different pots.

2 - C
Add up all the digits in each box in the first column to get the number in the second box.

3 - A = 13, B = 6
Half of the difference of the top two numbers.

4 - D
Each shape that appears in the smaller boxes is never repeated in the same row or column.

5 - A = 15, B = 26
Start in the top left segment and move clockwise. Add five for the first number, take away nine for the second and add seven for the final number.

6 - P
Move clockwise from the letter H, missing out one letter each step.

7 - 20
Add each pair of numbers.

8

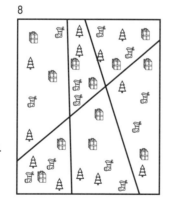

9 -
Cherries = 3
Lemon = 4
Banana = 5
Pear = 6

10 - 1 = K, 2 = R
Start at the top of each star and move in a clockwise direction. Miss out an extra letter each step.

11 - 30
Half of the value of each row.

12 - I
A is 95 minutes behind B.
C is 95 minutes behind I.

13 - 4
The numbers on the right hand side of the circle are squares of those in the opposite segments.

14 - J
A = 1, B = 2 etc.
The total of the first and third columns.

15 - A = 7, B = 4 & C = 8
The numbers in the righthand side of each circle are four times greater than those in the opposite segments.

16 - A = 127, B = 56
All other numbers are divisible by 9.

17 - 6
Letters of the alphabet, in order, turned 90 degrees and stretched. (Hold the page at a slant to get a better view.)

18 - 1
Add every feature from each box to make the third.

19

3S	1W	2E	2E	1S	3W
4S	1N	✱	2W	3E	5W
2E	2E	2S	1S	1E	2N
1E	1N	2N	1W	1W	1S
3E	2E	1S	1W	2N	1W
1N	1W	3E	2E	2N	2N

20 - 10 & 7
Moving from left to right, and alternating from top to bottom, odd numbers increase and even numbers decrease each step.

21 - B
Moving from top to bottom, left to right, each dot represents a number from one to nine. Simply add together the first two columns and rows to get the third.

22 - R
Midway between each pair of connecting letters.

23 - 16
The numbers indicate the position in the alphabet of the opposite letter.

24 - 14
Start at 3 and move clockwise. Add five then subtract two alternately.

25 - 3
Add up the numbers in each triangle, then add the digits of this answer together.

26 - P
Miss out an extra letter each step.

27 - 1
Add the numbers in each of the first two rows and columns to get the third.

28 - E
Letters in each of the top left corners increase by two. Those in the top right increase by three, in the bottom left by four and by five in the bottom right.

29 - 10
The numbers are double the value of the first six prime numbers, starting at the bottom and working up.

LEVEL 12

1 - 4
The features in the third boxes of each row and column are the opposite colour of the features in the previous box when they have not previously changed. If they have changed then they revert back to the colour in the first box.

2 - 21
Add up the digits in the upper two segments.
5 + 3 + 6 + 7 = 21

3 - A
Go forward three hours and then back one, keep repeating this until the end.

4 - 2
Multiply the bottom row and divide it by the top number.

5 - 2
Add up either the inner or outer numbers on all points of the triangle and divide by the number at the top.

6 - 1 = F & N, 2 = F & R, 3 = G & O
Miss out two letters then one alternately.

7 - 26
The numbers indicate the position in the alphabet of the letters in the opposite segment.

8 - 4

9 -

A	B	C	D	E
C	D	E	A	B
E	A	B	C	D
B	C	D	E	A
D	E	A	B	C

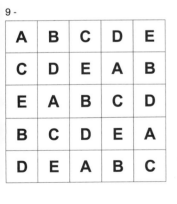

10 - 2
Add each double section. The numbers increase by one each step.

11 - 4
Multiply the numbers in the corresponding segments in the other circles.

12 - 1 = T, 2 = F
A = 1, B = 2 etc.
The numbers in Box 1 can be divided by 3, those in Box 2 can be divided by 4.

13 -

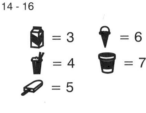

14 - 16

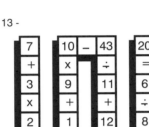

15 - 3
Move down from the top left corner adding the number directly beneath it, then move to the top of the next column and take this number away before repeating these steps.

16 - X
Start at D and move clockwise, missing out an extra letter each step.

17 - 6
Add up all the outer circles first and then add the digits of this answer together.
3 + 9 + 18 + 12 = 42, 4 + 2 = 6.

18 - A
The digits shown on each of the large watch faces all add up to 18.

19 - C
A = 1, B = 2 etc.
The numbers represent the first six prime numbers.

20 - 10
The difference between the top number and each of the bottom numbers added together.

21 - 26
The number in each box is the sum of the two boxes directly beneath it, minus one.

22 -

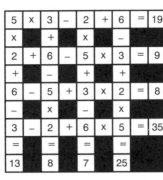

23 -

1	1	4	2	1	1	1
0	1	6	3	6	4	5
0	2	2	2	0	4	6
2	2	1	3	0	3	6
5	4	5	5	3	0	5
4	0	5	6	5	4	0
5	2	0	1	3	4	6
3	6	3	3	4	2	6

24 - J
Each letter is the same number of spaces into the alphabet from the beginning as the opposite letter is from the end.

25 - 865
Each column adds up to 3,333

26 - A
The number of sides on each shape increases by one each step.

27 - 75
Each ellipse contains the same multiples of 3, 4 & 5.

28 - J
A = 1, B = 2 etc.
Each pair of boxes adds up to 19.

29 - F
Each box contains the features in the boxes directly beneath it.

LEVEL 13

1 - D
The outer shape rotates by 45 degrees each step, the triangle by 90 degrees and the centre cross by 45 degrees.

2 -
He built giant snowballs out of the snow and used these to make a staircase to climb up.

3 - Y
A = 1, B = 2 etc.
Add up the letters of the connecting boxes.

4 - 8
It is the only shape with the same number of white and black circles within the large circle.

5 - A = 24, B = 56
Multiply the difference between each pair of numbers at every point of the triangle.

6 - 3
Start at the top left corner and move clockwise in a spiral pattern towards the centre. The seven different symbols are repeated in the same order every time.

7 -
1 = D, 2 = D & 3 = H
A = 1, B = 2 etc.
Multiply the top and bottom rows to get the centre row.

8 - 8
The value of the inner circle equals that of the outer circle.

9 - 9
Add the top and bottom rows together to get the centre row.

10 - 14 x 3 ÷ 6 + 47 - 15 = 39

11 -
A = 4 of Spades / B = 2 of Spades
C = 6 of Spades / D = 6 of Spades
E = 6 of Spades / F = 2 of Spades
Moving from left to right along each row, take away the value of each red card and add the value of each black one.

12 - W
Moving in a zig-zag pattern from left to right miss out one letter each step.

13 - 8
Add the second column to the first, then take away the third to get the fourth.

14 - A = 1, E = 9
Start in the top left corner and move in a spiral pattern towards the centre, take away the second number, add the third etc. to reach the centre box.

15 - T
Start with the centre letter and move clockwise throughout. Miss out two letters in the first grid, then three, then four and five in the last grid.

LEVEL 13

16 - A = 62, B = 90
Multiply each pair of numbers at the points of the triangles and add these together.

17 -
1 = 226, 2 = L & 3 = J
The numbers in the large ellipses represent the position in the alphabet of the adjacent letters. i.e. C = 3, G = 7 = 37.

18 - A = 13, B = 161
Start at the lowest number and move in a clockwise direction, doubling the preceding number, minus one.

19 - 2
Each diagonal line in the small boxes adds up to the same total.

20 - 11
The difference between the total of the top and bottom numbers and the left and right numbers.

21 - 5
Start in the top left circle and move left to right, top to bottom, work out the value of each coloured circle. Transfer the sum of the first two rows and columns to the third, starting again at the beginning when the end is reached.

22
```
11
21
```
The top row goes up by 2,3,4,5 & 6 each step. The bottom row increases by double this amount.

23 - J
There are two chains of letters. The first one, starting at A, jumps two letters each alternate tile. The second chain, starting at B, jumps one letter.

24 - B
The letter square reads the same going across as it does going down.

25 - 39
Double the preceding number, minus one, then minus two, minus three, etc.

26 - 1
Take away the corresponding segments in the second circle from the first to get the third.

27 - S & O
The bottom letter moves one place further forward from the top letter each step.

28 - 5
The total of each row decreases by 1 each step.

LEVEL 14

1 - B
The number of circles in each triangle matches the number of sides on each of the enclosed shapes.

2 - 8
The first columns and rows equal the sum of the second and third, minus the fourth.

3 - H
A = 1, B = 2, etc.
The sum of each column and row is 18.

4 -
```
7
16
```
The top row contains the first six prime numbers, the bottom row contains the first six square numbers.

5 - E
Starting in the top left corner of each box, add the value of the first symbol to the second to get the third.

6 - N
Every other consonant.

7 - 8
Multiply the first and third columns and add two.

8 - B
A = 1, B = 2 etc
The total value of each box is 50.

9 - 91
Start at the bottom and add 13, 15, 17 etc.

10 - 5

11 - 59
The digits in all the other balls all add up to 12.

12
A = 8, B = 7, C = 15 and D = 7
In each line the first and third numbers added together are double the value of the middle number.

13 - T
It is the only one that is repeated in both circles.

14 - A = 10, B = 11
Add the four outer numbers together and then add the digits of this answer together.

15 - 37
Start in the top left quarter and move in a clockwise direction. Multiply the first two numbers, take away the third to leave the fourth.

16 - F
The letters in the left-hand side of the circle are five places in front of those in the right-hand side.

17 - 90
Multiply each connecting line.

18 - M
All the other letters are one place further on in the alphabet than the vowels.

19 - 4
Move in a spiral pattern from the top left corner to the centre square. The white circle moves clockwise two points and the black circle moves anti-clockwise one point each step.

20 - E

21 - 20
The first and third numbers of each row and column equals the middle number.

22 - I
Circles become diamonds, squares become circles and diamonds become squares.

23 - 45

24 -
```
    3 3 8 9
x       2 0
  6 7 7 8 0
+   1 1 6 7
  6 8 9 4 7
```

25 -
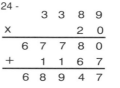

26 - 105
The value of the letters squared, plus five.

27 - 29
Each row and column adds up to 42.

28 - 61
It is the only number whose first digit is larger than the second.

29 - 7
A = 1, B = 2, etc.
Every column adds up to 50.

30 - T
The space between each tile increase by one each step, starting again at A whenever Z is reached.

31 - A = 2, B = 9
The numbers in each circle add up to 60.

LEVEL 15

1 - 5
The number of partitioned areas in the first column is equal to that of the other two columns added together.

2 - 485
Treble previous number and add 2.

3 - E S
Move down the first column and up the second, missing out one letter each step.

4 - 27
Each row adds up to the same total.

5 -
```
7 x 3 - 5 + 4 = 20
+     x   +   -
5 + 4 x 7 - 3 = 60
-   +   -   +
4 + 7 - 3 x 5 = 40
x       x   x
3 x 5 - 4 + 7 = 18
=   =   =   =
24  14  36  42
```

6 -

7 - D
Total of all digits displayed on each watch increases by four each step.

8 -
```
A F G P Z
F R C B T
G C U K Y
P B K I D
Z T Y D E
```
The puzzle reads the same going across as it does going down.

9 - 23
Multiply the numbers along the bottom row and add to the top.

10 - H (A = 1, B = 2, etc.)
Each box, when all the letters are added together, will total 49.

11 - 8
There are two sums in each cross. Add the first and second numbers of the middle column to get the third, or multiply the first and second numbers of the centre row to get the same answer.

12 - 2
The difference between the total of all odd numbers and even numbers.

13 - D
Each letter is the same number of places into the alphabet as its opposite letter is from the end.

LEVEL 15

14 - 6
The highest number in each column is the total of the other four.

15 - A = Q, B = J
Each centre letter is midway between the first and third letters of each row and column.

16 - 6
Multiply the top number by the bottom number. Multiply the left and right numbers, double the difference between the answers and write this in the centre box.

17 - D
The hour hand is in the right-hand side of each clock, the minute hand is on the left.

18 - 1 = H, 2 = G, 3 = B,
A = 1, B = 2 etc.
Multiply the top row by the bottom row to get the centre row.

19 - A = 4, B = 6 & C = 10
The difference between the top numbers and the multiplied total of the bottom row.

20 - 23
Start in the top left segment and move in a clockwise direction, subtracting the first digit each step.

21 - H
Starting at A and moving anti-clockwise, the first eight letters having only straight lines are used.

22 - 4
Add up all the digits. Each connecting line adds up to 17.

23 - C
The number of legs on each creature continues the sequence of 4, 2, 0, 4, 2.

24 - U
It is the only letter of the alphabet not used in the grid.

25 - 13
Both halves of the circle equal 79.

26 - 7
The top left number in each box is the average of the other three numbers.

27 - 17
Add together the corresponding numbers in the other three boxes.

28 - M
Each pair of opposite letters are 11 letters apart.

29 - X
The outer ring contains every third letter in a random pattern. The inner ring contains the next letter on from each of these, although not in order.

30 - A = 2, B = 1, C = 4 & D = 3

LEVEL 16

1 - F
Start at the top and move downwards left to right. Rotate the box 90° each time, taking away one feature every other step.

2 - 88

3 - 7
Move along each line doing the same sum. e.g. 9 = 6 + 7 - 4

4 - One solution is:

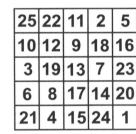

5 -

25	22	11	2	5
10	12	9	18	16
3	19	13	7	23
6	8	17	14	20
21	4	15	24	1

6 - 4
The black dots represent consecutive numbers. (Turn the page upside down at look at it flat.)

7 - 5
Remove the lowest and highest numbers each time. Write the remaining numbers down in the opposite direction.

8 - 1 = P, 2 = J
Write down the letters in order and move forward an extra letter each time.

9 - 32
Start in the top left circle and move clockwise, take away the second number, add the third and multiply it by the fourth.

10 - D
On each of the larger watch faces the minutes are four times greater than the hours shown.

11 - 9
Multiply each row by 5, then 6, then 7 etc. etc.

12 - 51
Reverse the numbers shown in the larger ellipses and add them together. (35 + 16 = 51)

13 - 9
The centre column is the total of all the numbers to the left, minus the total of all those on the right.

14 - E
It is a vertical mirror image of C.

15 - M
A=1, B = 2 etc.
Add the numbers from the corresponding sections of the first two boxes and write the answer, as a letter, in the third, returning to A whenever Z is reached.

16 - 21
Multiply the top number by the bottom number, add the left-hand number before taking away the number in the right-hand box.

17 - B
All other aliens have been created using the same shapes.

18 - 25
The total of each group of numbers increases by 25 each time.

19 - J
Start in the top left corner and move anti-clockwise. Go back three spaces each time.

20 - G
The value of the red cards in each row and column is equal to that of the black cards.

21 - N
A = 1, B = 2 etc.etc.
Starting at F and moving anti-clockwise keep multiplying each number by 2. Write the answers, as letters, returning to A whenever Z is reached.

22 - 48
Multiply the three digits in the first box. (8 x 1 x 6 = 48)

23 - 1
The shape in each of the bottom boxes will, when added to the shape above, form a square.

24 -

25 - 142
The difference between the numbers is 2^2, 3^2, 4^2, 5^2 etc.etc.

26 - 44
Start at 8 and move in a clockwise direction. Add six for the second number, eight for the third, then ten, etc.etc.

27 -

7	2	9	16
13	12	3	6
4	5	14	11
10	15	8	1

28 - 2
Start in the bottom left corner and move clockwise. Multiply the first number by the second, then add the third to get the fourth number.

29 - 9
Add up the odd numbers in each square.

30 - O
Each row and column contains a different vowel.

SOLUTIONS ~ SOLUTIONS ~ SOLUTIONS ~ SOLUTIONS

1 - 5
All other shapes rotate 90° from the previous one except No 5 which rotates 180°.

2 - 5
There are two chains of numbers, the first chain, starting at 1 increases by 1 every other tile and the second chain, starting at 3, increases by 2 every other tile.

3 - D
Every domino number (including blank) appears once in each row and column.

4 - 45
Each box contains a number that is the total of the two boxes directly beneath it, minus two.

5 -

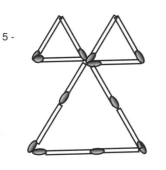

6 - H

7 - 3
The number of small shapes inside the larger ones corresponds with the number of sides on each of the smaller shapes.

8 - 23
The bottom number is one quarter the value of the largest number, minus the other one.

9 - No
There is not information given to help find the exact answer.

10 -

Starting in the top right corner, the square reads the same across as it does going down.

11 - 9
Add up each pair of numbers in every segment. Moving in a clockwise direction the totals in the right-hand side of the circle are 12, 10, 8 & 6 different from the totals of the opposite segments.

12 - D
Starting at J and moving anti-clockwise, the letters increase by 10 each step, returning to A whenever Z is reached.

13 - J
A = 1, B = 2 etc. etc.
Each set of four opposite letters adds up to 26.

14 - E
The digits on each watch face add up to 15.

15 - V
One letter on from each vowel in the alphabet.

16 - 3
Add up the four outer numbers and then add up the digits of this answer.

17 - 5
Matching pairs are; 1 & 6, 2 & 7, 3 & 4 and 8 & 9.

18 - 92
Start at the top and move anti-clockwise, multiply the first two numbers, add the third and then subtract the first number again.

19 - X
The letters in the third column are double the number of spaces away from the second as the second is from the first.

20 - 16
There are two chains of numbers, both moving down the first column, up the second, down the third etc. etc.
The first chain is made up of odd numbers and appears in every other box, the second chain, made up of all even numbers, alternates with the first.

21 - A
A = 1, B = 2 etc. etc.
The letters in each star add up to 50.

22 - 8
Multiply the top two numbers and take away the total of the bottom two numbers.

23 - 1 = T, 2 = M
The other letters spell out the name of Michael Douglas.

24 - 8
Add all five numbers together to get the square of the centre figure.

25 - 23
Starting at the bottom number and moving clockwise, add 2, then 3 and then 4.

26 - A = 0, B = 6, C = 1, D = 9
Multiply the top two numbers of each column and write the last digit of the answer in the bottom box.

27 - C
The square moves two places anti-clockwise each step, the triangle moves four places clockwise and the circle is placed between the two of them.

28 - 1535
Times shown on a twenty-four hour clock, moving forward 75 minutes each step.

29 - 63 moves.

30 - You cannot dig half a hole - as soon as you start it is a hole!

1 - U
Z = 1, Y = 2
Each of the centre letters is equal to the total of the first and third letters in each row and column.

2 - R
Starting at B and moving in a clockwise spiral pattern towards the centre, move forward two spaces each step.

3 - Z
Every letter has got three straight lines.

4 - E
The letters spell out CHRISTOPHER REEVE

5 - 3
Start in the top left corner and move diagonally from left to right. The symbols appear in the same running order throughout.

6 - E
The number of straight edges on the letter V is two less than than the total in the letter Y.
E has got two more edges than N.

7 - 5
The grid includes
1 1 (1x1),
4 2's (2x2)
9 3's (3x3)
16 4's (4x4)
25 5's (5x5)
36 6's (6x6)
49 7's (7x7)

8 - B
The letters move backwards 2,3,4,5 & 6 spaces each step.

9 - G
A & C are the same, as are B & F, D & I and E & H.

10 - 9
The top boxes are equal to the bottom box multiplied by thirteen.

11 - F
A = 1, B = 2 etc. etc.
All multiples of three.

12 - 15
When written in Roman Numerals, the number of straight lines used in each line across is twelve.

13 - 4
Half of the previous number, minus two.

14 -

Moving down the first column and up the second, go back two, forward three, back four, forward five, back six, etc.etc.

15 -
A = 9 - Multiply the bottom box by three and add two.
B = 36 - Divide the top box by seven then multiply that answer by three.
C = 5 - Square the bottom box and add three.

16
1 = S, 2 = V
All other letters are made up of straight and curved lines.

17 - 19
Each line across the three grids (top, middle and bottom) equals exactly 100.

18 - B
Add together the digits that the hands of each clock are pointing to. In each case the total is 13.

19 - 5
Starting at C and moving anti-clockwise alternate between numbers and letters, adding an extra 1 each step. Return to A whenever Z is reached.

20 - B
Add up the numbers on the bottom row and subtract the top one. Write the letter of the alphabet which is represented by the final digit of this sum in the centre.

21 - 5
Each of the three coloured circles add up to 36.

22 - O
A = 1, B = 2, etc. (start over again at Z) beginning at A and moving counterclockwise, differences between letters follow sequence 2, 4, 8, 16

23 - 19
Two chains of letters, prime numbers and square numbers, put into numerical order.

24 - 7
Add the first and last boxes of each row and column, then take away three to get the middle number.

25 - 3
Starting in the top left corner and moving in a clockwise spiral pattern towards the centre, each star rotates 30° every step.

26 - E

27 - 6
Add up each pair of corner numbers, across and down, and write the answer in the centre box opposite.

1 - G
The pyramid will spell out the name GOLDIE HAWN.

2 -

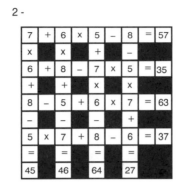

7	+	6	x	5	−	8	=	57
x				x		+		−
6	+	8	−	7	x	5	=	35
+				+		x		x
8	−	5	+	6	x	7	=	63
−				−		−		+
5	x	7	+	8	−	6	=	37
=				=		=		=
45				46		64		27

3 - 6
In every row and column four consecutive numbers appear in random order.

4 - 3
Five vowels appear in every row and column.

5 - 16
Starting at 4 and moving in a clockwise direction add three to every prime number.

6 - 8191
The position in the alphabet of each letter joined together and written in reverse order.

7 - T
A chain of letters containing only straight lines.

8 - 4
Add together the second and third rows and columns, then add the digits of this answer together so that a single figure is reached. Write this in the first box.

9 - P
Each letter is the same number of places in from one end of the alphabet as the diagonally opposite letter is from the other.

10 - 2
Square numbers minus its root.
e.g. 7 x 7 = 49 - 7 = 42

11 - 1
Take the top row away from the middle row to get the third.

12 - 41122314
The numbers indicate the total of each numeral in the previous row. i.e. in the penultimate row there are 4 x 1, 1 x 2, 2 x 3 and 1 x 4.

13 - A = 73, B = 54
Multiply the top and bottom numbers, then the left and right numbers. Add these two answers together and write this, in reverse order, in the centre.

14 - 55
25 x 1, 16 x 4, 9 x 9, 4 x 16 and 1 x 25.

15 - 94
Multiply the first and last digits in the first column by the centre number.
i.e. 526 = 112 (56 x 2 = 112)

16 - F
A = 1, B = 2 etc. etc.
Take away the the third row and column from the first to get the second.

17 - S
When written in capitals it is the only letter that cannot be filled in.
e.g. A B D O P Q R

18 - 8
Work across the rows doing the same sum.
4 x 3 + 2 - 8 = 6
7 x 1 + 6 - 5 = 8

19 - F
Moving from left to right and top to bottom, the black and white ellipses move clockwise each step, whilst the grey ellipse moves anti-clockwise.

20 -

21 - 12
A = 1, B = 2 etc. etc.
The value of all the numbers is
equal to that of all the letters.

22 - I
A = 1, B = 2 etc. etc.
Add up the letters in the corresponding points of the first two
stars. Write the answer, as a
letter, in the third star, one point
clockwise from the original
position.

23 - 4
Add up the four outer numbers
and divide it by 4.

24 - B
Alternate between black and red
cards, taking away the value of
the second, adding the third,
etc. etc.
10 - 7 + 8 - 9 + 3 = 5

25 - 12
The centre box of each row and
column is the total of both boxes
on either side.

26 -

1 -
A = 3 - Add the top row to the
bottom row to get the middle row.

B = 6 - Take away the middle row
from the top to get the bottom row.

C = 1: 9 + 4 - 1 - 1 - 3 = 8

D = 9: 9 = 8 + 6 - 2 + 1 - 4

2 - D
The number of edges on the
shapes inside the hexagon is
the same on the top half as it
is on the bottom half.

3 - F
Work from top to bottom,
adding together the letters
in the top left and bottom
right segments to reach
the answers in the
corresponding segments
in the bottom grid.
Then, for the top right and
bottom left solutions, subtract
the sum of the second and
third from the first and write
the answers in the
corresponding segments in
the bottom grid.

4 - 9
Starting at the segment
containing No 10, work
clockwise, increase the
difference of the two
numbers in each segment
by an extra 3 each step.

5 - Any one of 66, 75, 84 or 93.
Add together the digits in
every row and column to
get a total of 20.

6 - 4
Add together the three numbers
that are not part of another box
and divide it by four to get the
final number.

7 - 2
Start in the top portion of each
square and take away the other
three numbers. The centre
number is double the final figure.

8 - N
The letters will spell out the name
MADONNA

9 - P
Start in the outer ring and move
clockwise. Go one step towards
the centre each step and move
forward four letters of the
alphabet until you reach the
inner ring.

10 - 30
The number of days in each of the
first six months of the year.

11 - 650
Add together the digits in the first
and third columns. Multiply these
two answers together to get the
middle box.

12 - 4
A sequence of five symbols
are used diagonally from
left to right every other row
starting in the top left corner.
The spaces are then filled
with the same five symbols
moving from left to right, top
to bottom.

13 - E
The letters spell out the name
CHARLIE SHEEN

14 - H
A = 1, B = 2 etc. etc.
Add the top and bottom letters
together and then the left and
right letters. The centre letter
is equal to the difference in the
first puzzle, double the difference
in the second, three times in the
third and four times the difference
in the last puzzle.

15 - 10
The centre figure is the difference
between the total of the odd and
even numbers.

16 - 4
Starting at the top, multiply each
line by 7 to get the next line down.

17 - 4
Multiply the first column by the
fourth and write the answer in
the middle two boxes, putting a
separate digit in each box.

18 -
A = S
A = 1, B = 2 etc. etc.
Start in the top left corner
and move counterclockwise
in a spiral pattern towards
the centre. Multiply the first
letter by two, take away three
and keep repeating until the
end.

B = Q
A = 1, B = 2 etc. etc.
Start in the bottom right corner and
move clockwise in a spiral pattern
towards the centre. Multiply the
first letter by two, take away one
and keep repeating until the end.

19 - 58
Join together the top and bottom
digits then the left and right. Add
these two together and put the
answer backwards in the centre.
i.e. 21 + 37 = 85

20 - G
Every row and column contains
the same four grids.

BRAVO!